C000291778

PORTSMOUTH

ESTATE PUBLICATIONS
Bridewell House,
Tenterden, Kent.
TN30 6EP
Tel: 01580 764225

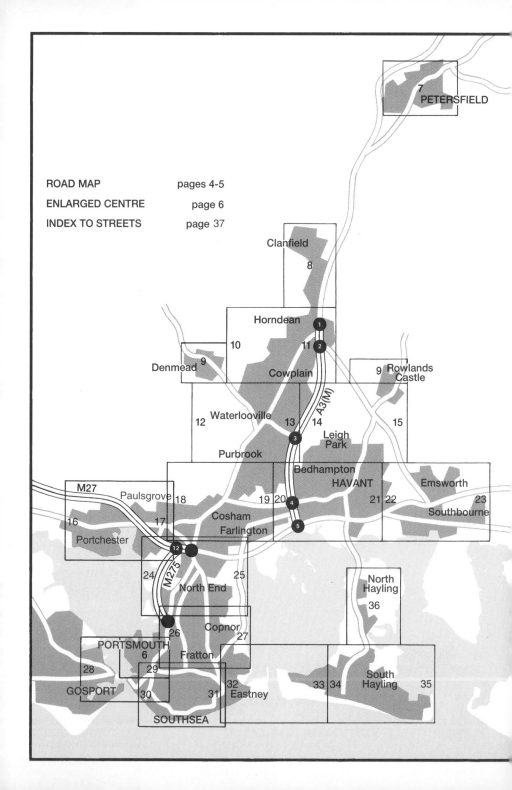

PORTSMOUTH

HAVANT · PETERSFIELD · SOUTHSEA

One-way Street	→
Car Park	℗
Place of Worship	✚
Post Office	●
Public Convenience	Ⓒ
Pedestrianized	▨

Scale of street plans 4 inches to 1 mile
Unless otherwise stated

Street plans prepared and published by ESTATE PUBLICATIONS, Bridewell House, TENTERDEN, KENT, and based upon the ORDNANCE SURVEY maps with the sanction of the Controller of H. M. Stationery Office.

The publishers acknowledge the co-operation of the local authorities of towns represented in this atlas

Estate Publications 69 P   ISBN 0 86084 946 5   © Crown Copyright 398713

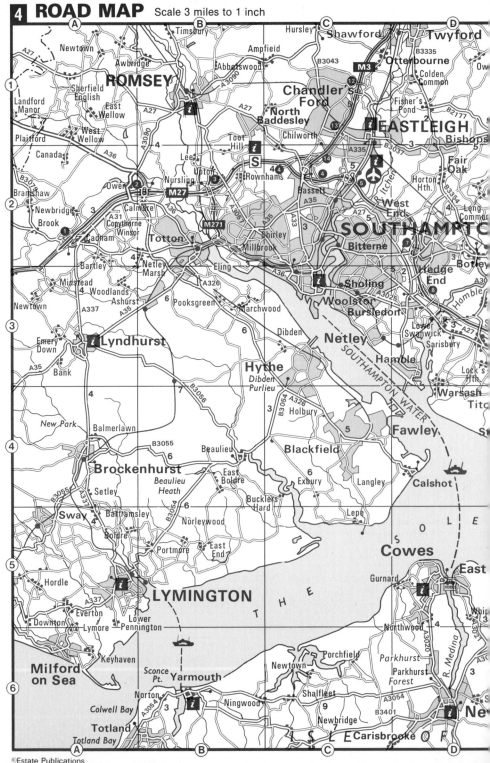

4 ROAD MAP Scale 3 miles to 1 inch

©Estate Publications

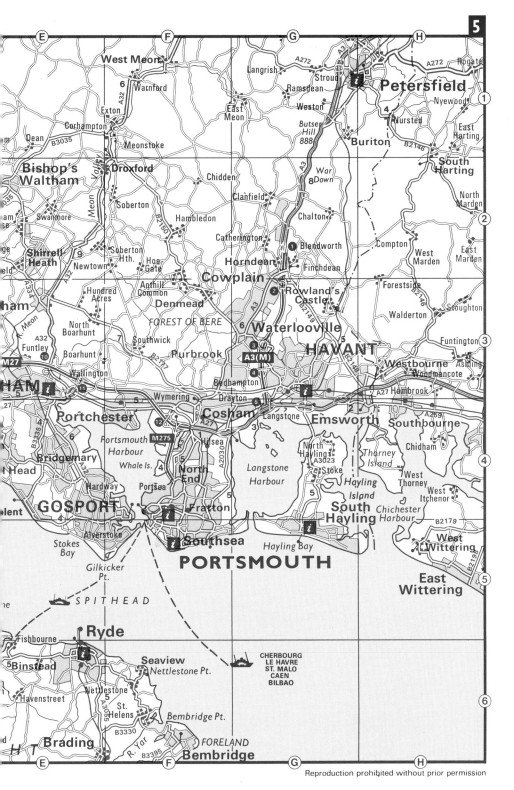

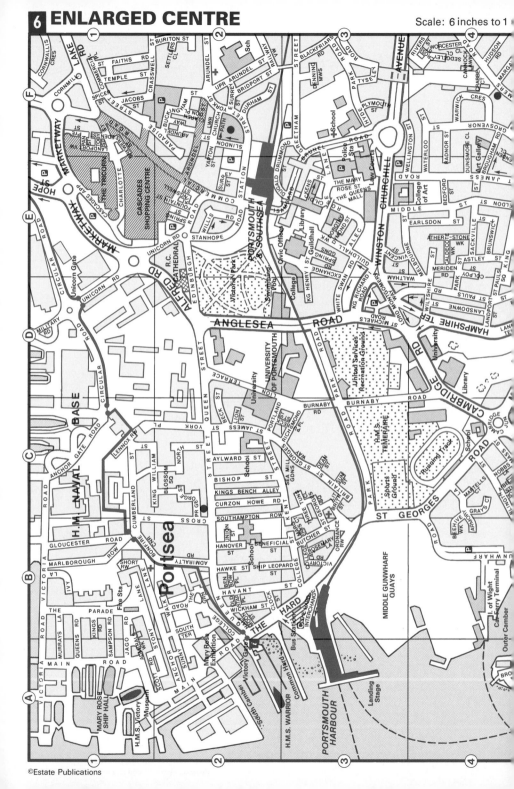

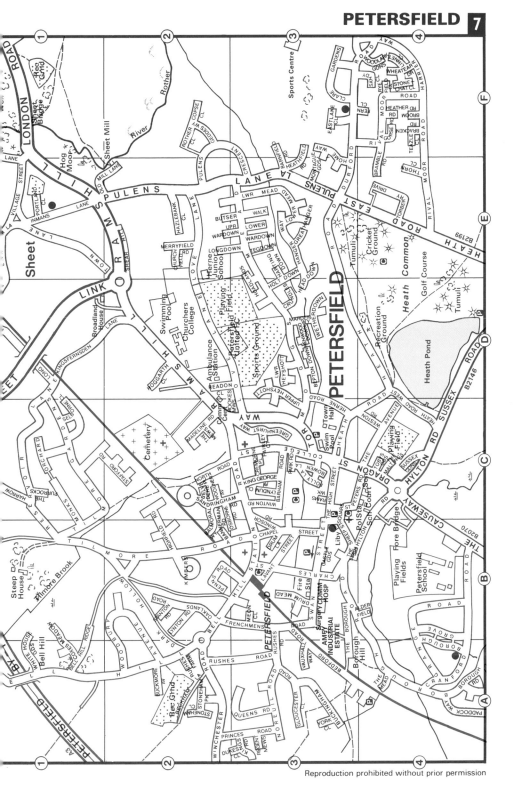

Denmead

ROWLANDS CASTLE

©Estate Publications

Furzeley Corner

Piper's Hill Wood

PIPERS WOOD INDUSTRIAL PARK

Sheepwash Coppice

Greatplant Wood

Shorts Coppice

Lattle Coppice

Duneland Coppice

Wares Coppice

Plant Farm

Fareham Garden

Newlandsmoor Coppice

Mallins Plantation

Mallins Coppice

Parland Coppice

Cooper Hill

Drivers Coppice

Southwick House

Astordmoor Coppice

Marrelsmoor Row

Broomground Coppice

Poswell Coppice

Marrelsmoor Coppice

Purbrook

©Estate Publications

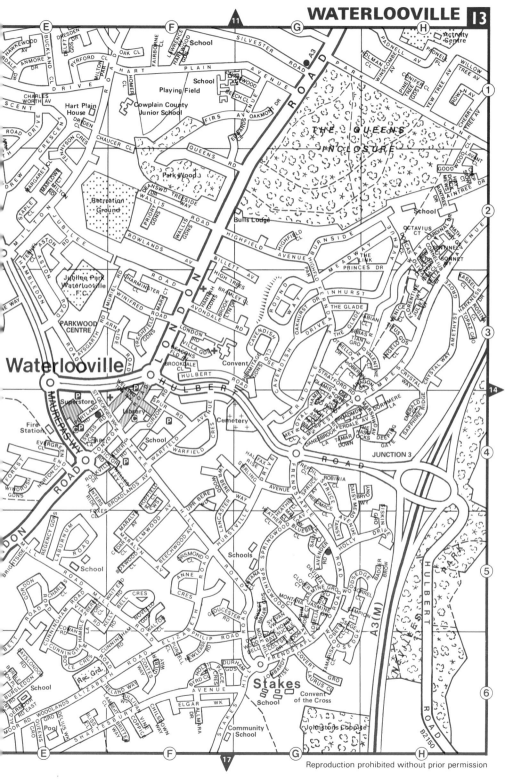

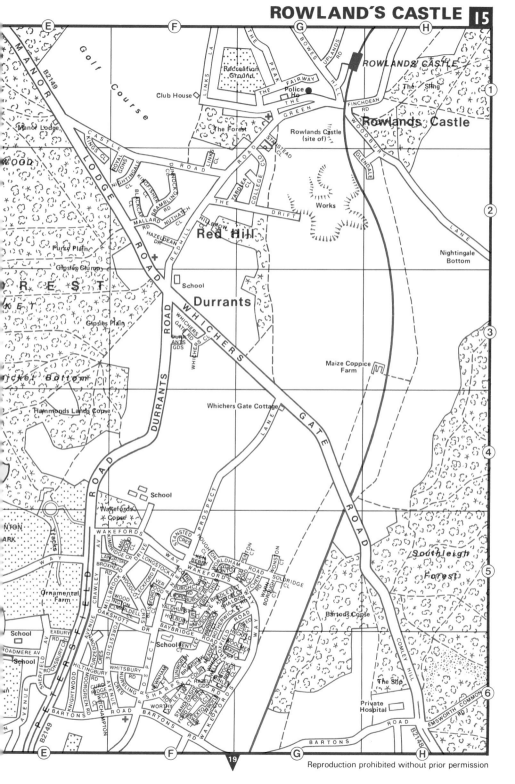

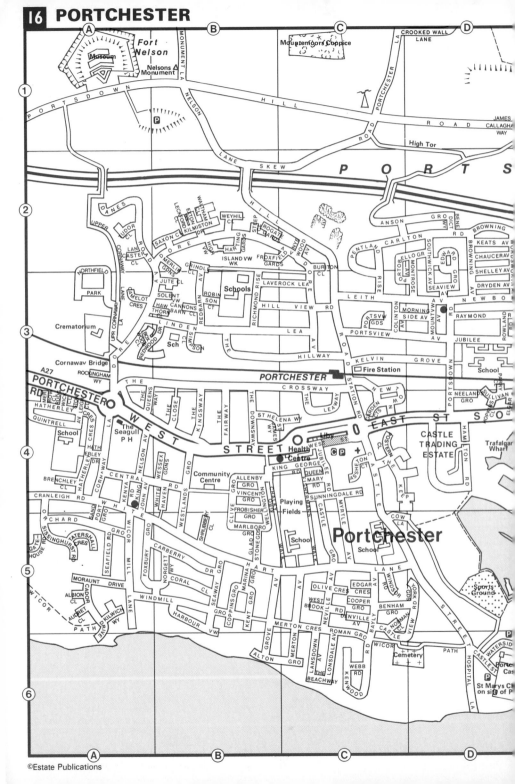

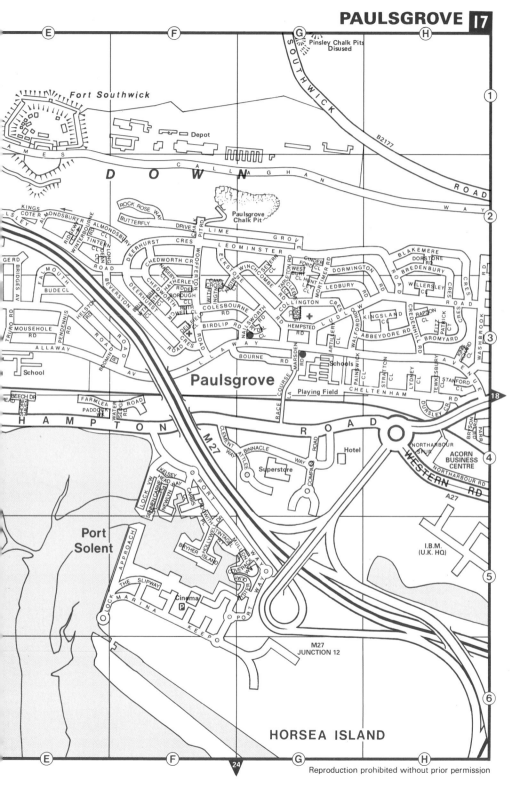

Pinsley Chalk Pits
Disused

Fort Southwick

Depot

DOWN

CALLAGHAN ROAD WAY

SOUTHWICK

B2177

KINGS
COTER
MONDSBURY
ALMONDSBURY CL
WATERBOURNE
RIDLEY
TINTERN
CLOEN
ROAD

ROCK ROSE WAY
BUTTERFLY
CHALK
PIT RD
DRIVE
Paulsgrove
Chalk Pit

LIME GROVE

LEOMINSTER

DEERHURST CRES
CHEDWORTH CROFT
WOOFFERTON
ELKSTONE
WINCHCOMBE

BLAKEMERE
DORSTONE
RD
BREDENBURY

HATHERLEY
CHEDWORTH CL
DERBY
BORDUGH
COWELL CL
DELPER CL
BIRDLIP RD

CAM
CROSS
KINGTONE
MALSTONE
WESTERN
CL
FORD CL
ARTICLE
CL HENT
CL
MORTIMER RD
DORMINGTON

WILLERSLEY
CRES

GERD
BRIDGES AV
FALMOUTH
BUDE CL
BEVERSTON RD
DEERHURST
COLESBOURNE RD

LEDBURY
COLLINGTON CRES
HEMPSTED RD

KINGSLAND
CREDENHILL RD
ABBEYDORE RD
RAPSON
CL
BROMYARD
FELTZ
PATRICK
CT

WASHBROOK

TRURO
RD
MOUSEHOLE
RD
PENDENNIS
RD
HELSTON RD
BROMLING
ROAD
ROAD
ROAD

NAILSWORTH
NAILSTON CL
HEMPSTED RD
ARTILLERY
CL
LUDLOW
WALFORD
PAINSWICK CL

ABBEYDORE RD

ALLAWAY

School

FARMLEA

BEVERSTON RD
CRES

BOURNE RD
MARSDEN RD

Schools

STRATTON
CL
LYDNEY
CL
STANFORD
CL
CHELTENHAM
DURSLEY

TEWKSBURY
STANFORD
CL
R D

18

BEECH DR
FARMLEA
PADDOCK
WK
WATER
SEDGE
ROAD

Paulsgrove

RACE
COURSE
LA
Playing Field

HAMPTON ROAD WESTERN RD

M27
CLEMENT
WAY
ATTLEE
WAY
BINNACLE WAY
PORT
CROWITH
SENEN
CARBIS
NEWKIN
KELSEY
HEAD WAY
LOCK VW

COMPASS WAY
Superstore

Hotel
NORTHARBOUR
SPUR
ACORN
BUSINESS
CENTRE
NORTHARBOUR RD

A27

BRYHER ISLAND
VINTAGE
OVERTON
FOSTER
WAY
PORT WAY
KEEP

**Port
Solent**

APPROACH
THE SLIPWAY
LOCK MARINA

Cinema
P

I.B.M.
(U.K. HQ)

M27
JUNCTION 12

HORSEA ISLAND

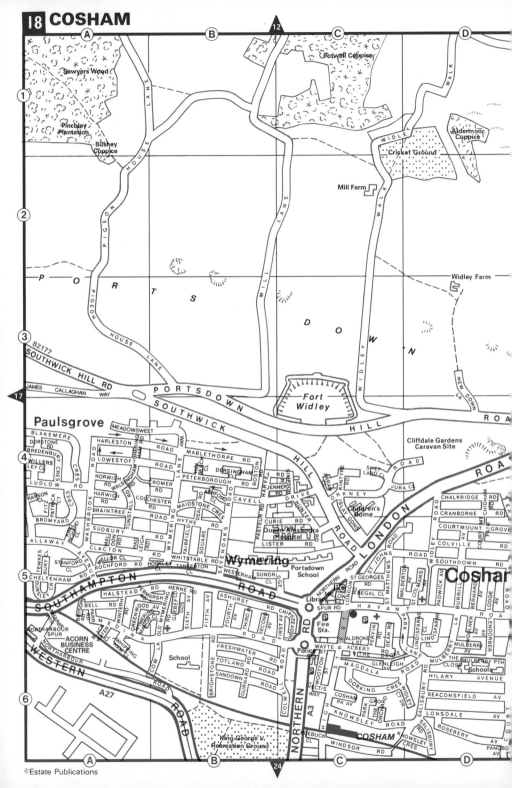

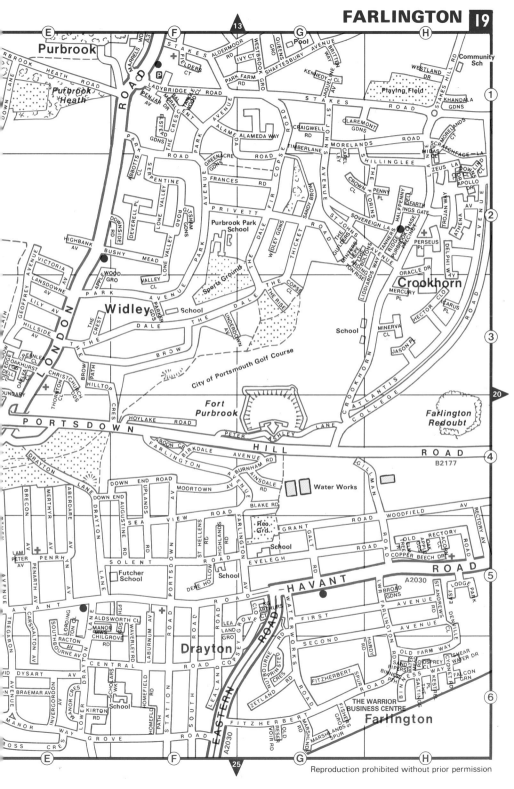

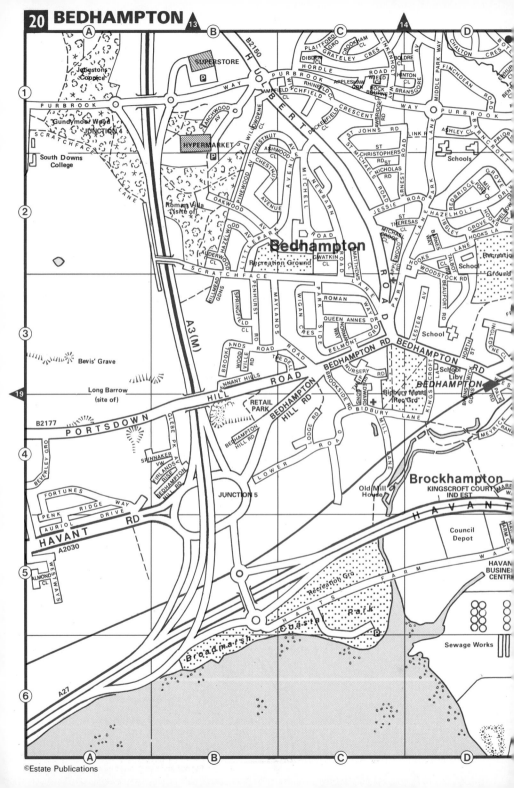

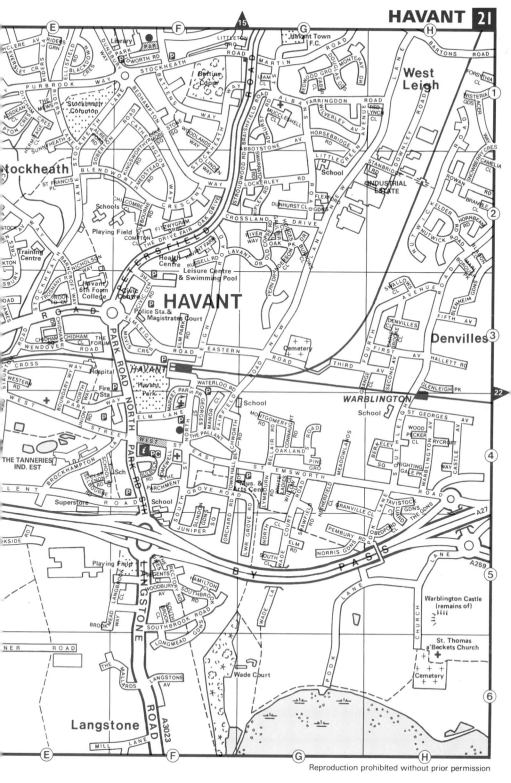

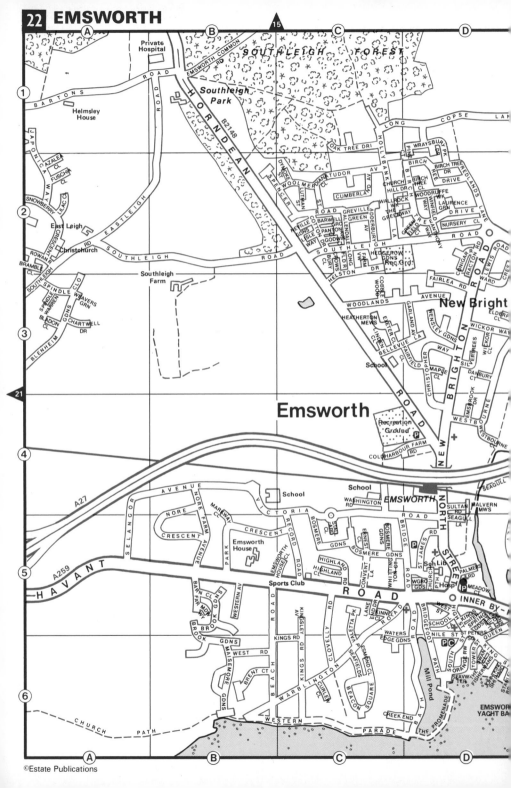

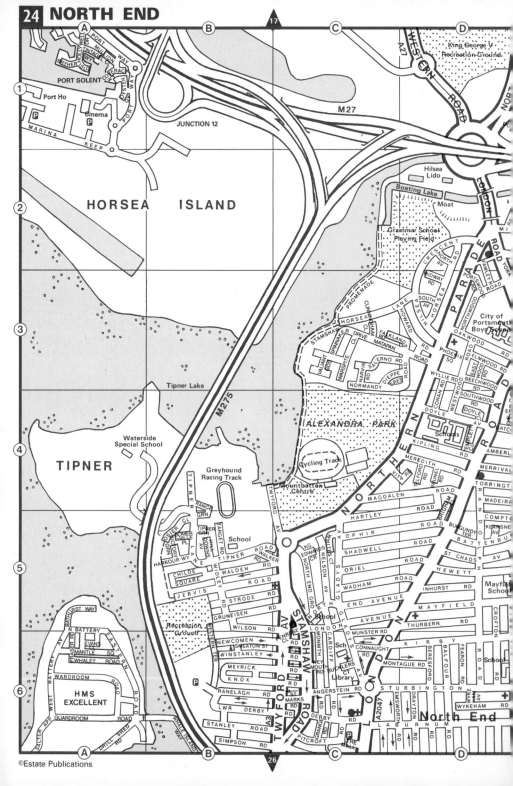

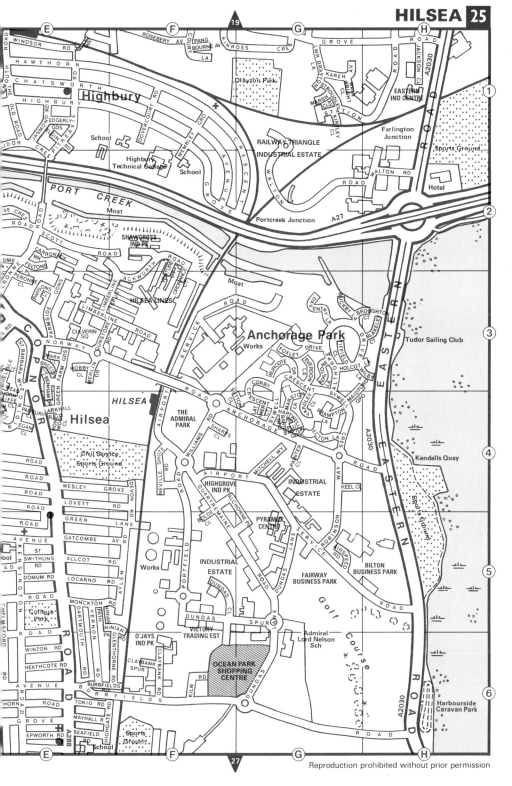

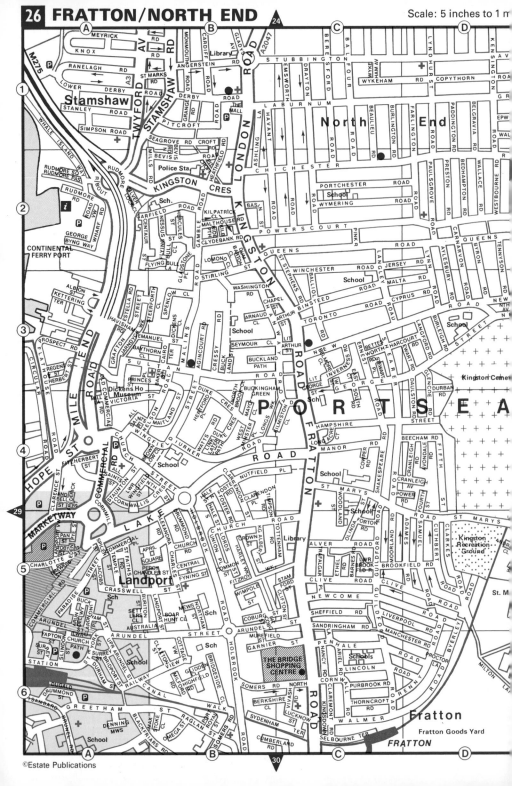

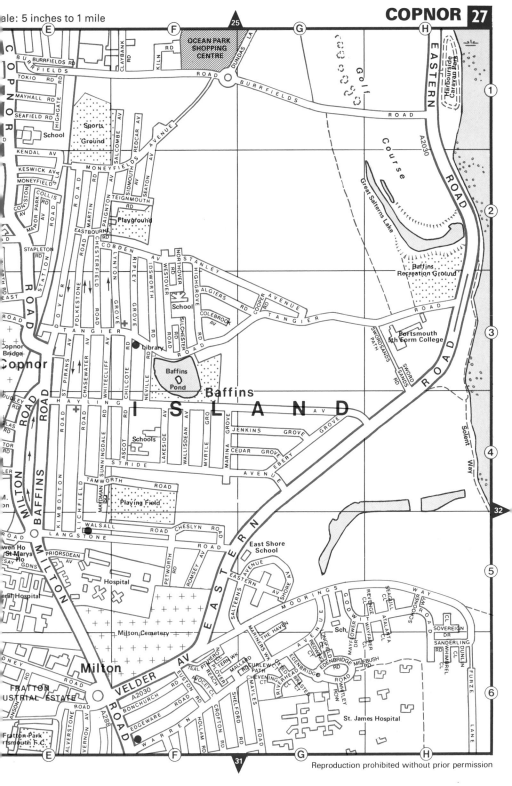

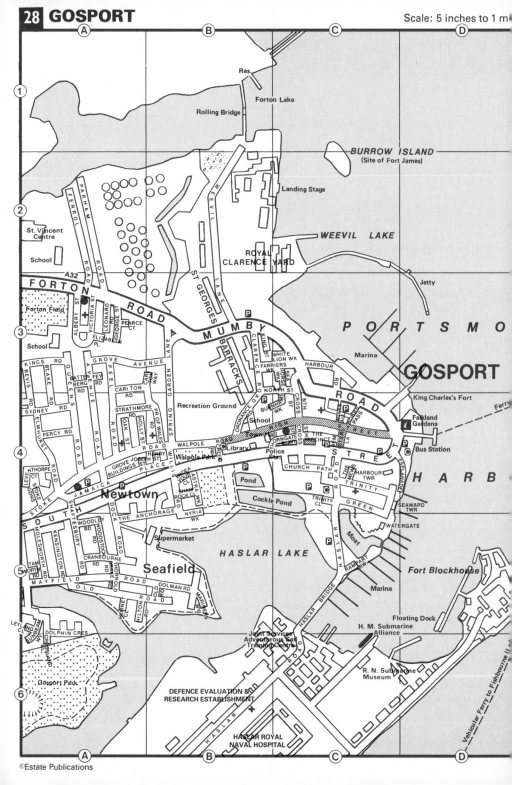

Res.

Forton Lake

Rolling Bridge

BURROW ISLAND
(Site of Fort James)

Landing Stage

St. Vincent Centre

School

WEEVIL LAKE

A32

ROYAL CLARENCE YARD

FORTON ROAD

Forton Field

School

PARHAM ROAD
FERROL ROAD
ROAD

MUMBY

BARRACKS

ST GEORGES LANE
WEEVIL LANE

KINGS RD
BEVIS
BLAKE
RD
SYDNEY RD
ELMHURST
PERCY RD

QUEENS
BATTEN
BERG
RD
FEY
RD

ALBERT ST
VICTORIA ST
LEONARD
GEORGE ST
ELIZABETH
PL

GROVE
PEEL
AVENUE
CARLTON
WAY
STRATHMORE
RD
OAK ST
HOLLY ST
ROAD

PEARCE CT

SPRING GARDEN LANE

WHITE LION WK
KING ST
CLARENCE
FARRIERS
WK
NORTH ST
BURHILL WK

CARLTON

P

Marina

PORTSMO

GOSPORT

King Charles's Fort

Falkland Gardens

HARBOUR RD

Recreation Ground

Ferry

School

Town Hall

Library

Bus Station

Police Sta.

HARBOUR TWR

ESPLANADE

HARB

NTHORPE RD
LEVE
CT
STOKE
GDNS
STOKE
SOUTH

JAMAICA
Newtown

GROVE
JOSEPH ST
BUILDINGS
PLACE

WALPOLE

Walpole Park

THE PRECINCT

CHURCH PATH
TRINITY

TRINITY CL

GREEN

SEAWARD TWR

SHAFTESBURY

WOODLEY RD
MOLESWORTH RD
KENSINGTON RD

DOCK
THE ANCHORAGE

Pond

Cockle Pond

Pond

WATERGATE

Supermarket

HASLAR LAKE

HASLAR BRIDGE ROAD

Fort Blockhouse

Marina

TAM
WORTH RD
MAYFIELD
RD

CRANBOURNE RD
THORNE RD
OLD
ROAD

Seafield

DOLMAN RD
WALTERS

RAMPART ROW

Moat

LEYLAND
CL
SUNBEAM
CRESLAND
DOLPHIN CRES

HORNET RD
HILTON RD
OLD ROAD

Floating Dock

H. M. Submarine Alliance

R. N. Submarine Museum

Gosport Park

JOINT Services Adventurous Sail Training Centre

DEFENCE EVALUATION & RESEARCH ESTABLISHMENT

HASLAR ROYAL NAVAL HOSPITAL

Vehicular Ferry to Fishbourne

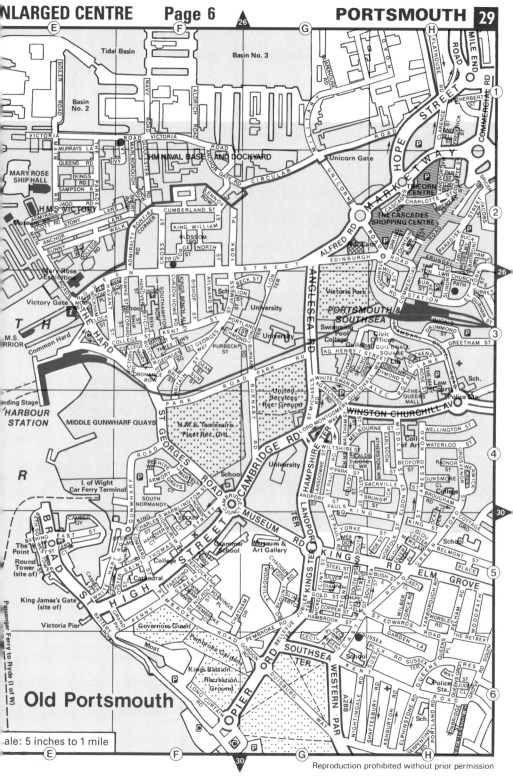

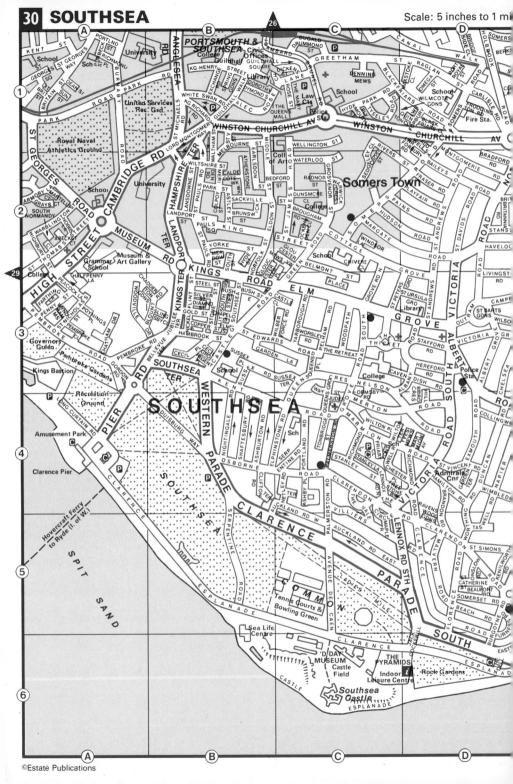

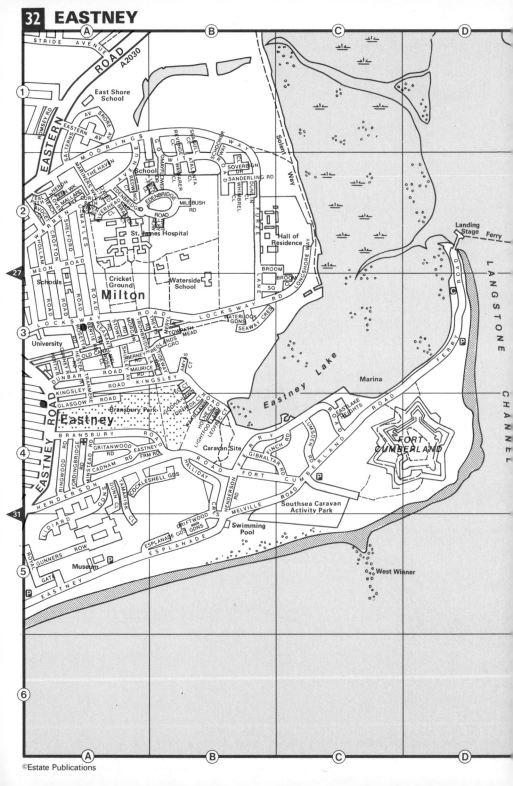

STRIDE AVENUE
EASTERN ROAD A2030
RDMSEY RD
East Shore School
SHORE AV
SALTERNS
EASTERN AV
MOORINGS
SEAGULL
SCHOONER WAY
SOVEREIGN OR
SANDERLING RD
SCHOOL
REDWING
EDENBRIDGE CL
EDENBRIDGE ROAD
MILEBUSH RD
WHIMBREL CL
FURZE
Solent Way
St. James Hospital
Hall of Residence
THE HAVEN
MARINERS WK
MALLARD
CURLEW
CHURCH PATH
AVOCET
CHEVERTON
HERON
SHELFORD
CROFTON
PLOVER WK
SNAYLES
RREN CL
HOLLAND
MEON
CROFTON
ROAD
LOCKSWAY
Schools
BROOM LANE
BROOM SQ
BROOM CL
Cricket Ground
Milton
Waterside School
LOCKSWAY
Longshore Way
WATERLOO GDNS
SEAWAY CRES
University
LOCKSWAY
ROAD
TOWPATH MEAD
MERVI
TOWPATH
PLEASANT
STOWE
MORGAN
ROONBRIDGE
BASSETT
BERTIE ROAD
CHESTER ROAD
OLD CANAL
REDLANDS
GRO
AMYS CT
ABERNEY RD
SHIRLEY
MAURICE RD
TRAINMERE
DUNBAR
ROAD
BERTH
ROAD
KINGSLEY
ROAD
KINGSLEY
GLASGOW ROAD
Eastney
Bransbury Park
GOODWIN
TOREFIELD
LIGHTFOOT
HOLE LANE
WAKEFIELD
LEOFRIC CL
LANDPORT
Landing Stage
Ferry
C
FERRY ROAD
P
LANGSTONE
Marina
EASTLAKE HEIGHTS
LUMSDEN ROAD
FORT CUMBERLAND
CHANNEL
Eastney Lake
EASTNEY ROAD
BRANSBURY ROAD
RINGWOOD RD
FORDINGBRIDGE
MINSTEAD
CADNAM
RD
EASTNEY FRM RD
EASTNEY FRM RD
HENDERSON
LLGIARD GDNS
TAMARISK CL
COCKLESHELL GDNS
GRITANWOOD RD
HALLIDAY
ROAD
HENDERSON RD
FORT CUMBERLAND ROAD
FINCH RD
GIBRALTAR RD
FERRY RD
MELVILLE RD
Caravan Site
P
Southsea Caravan Activity Park
P
DRIFTWOOD GDNS
ESPLANADE GDS
ESPLANADE
GUNNERS ROW
ROYAL GATE
Museum
P
EASTNEY
P
Swimming Pool
West Winner

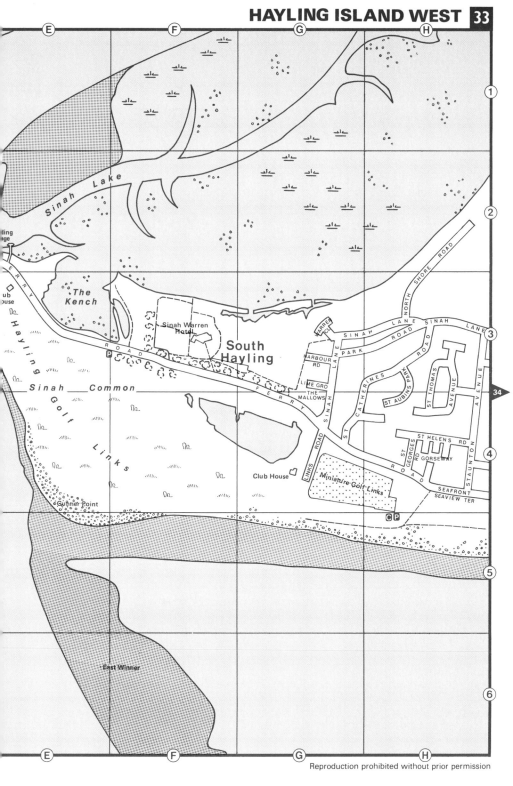

Sinah Lake

The Kench

Sinah Warren Hotel

South Hayling

Hayling

Sinah Common

Golf Links

Gunner Point

Club House

Miniature Golf Links

East Winner

WARREN RD

SINAH LANE PARK

HARBOUR RD

LIME GRO

THE MALLOWS

FERRY ROAD

LINKS ROAD

SINAH ROAD

ST CATHERINES RD

ST AUBINS PARK

ST THOMAS RD

STAUNTON AVENUE

AVENUE

NORTH SHORE ROAD

SINAH LANE

SINAH LANE

ST GEORGES ROAD

ST HELENS RD

GORSEWAY

SEAFRONT

SEAVIEW TER

CP

34

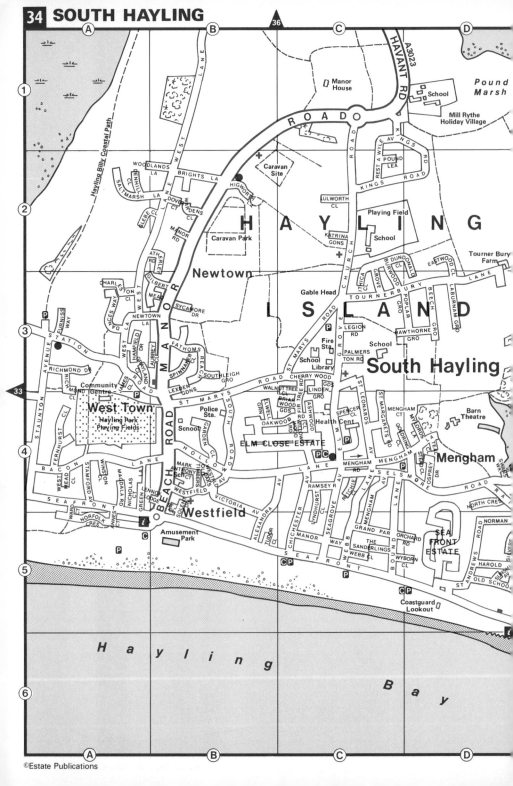

Pound Marsh

Mill Rythe Holiday Village

Manor House

School

A3023

HAVANT RD

ROAD

KINGS ROAD

KINGS RD

WYLE AV

REST A

POUND LEA

Caravan Site

LULWORTH CL

Playing Field

School

H A Y L I N G

Caravan Park

KATRINA GDNS

WOODLANDS LA

BRIGHTS LA

HIGWORTH

DENHILL CL

SALTMARSH LA

GLEBE CL

DOVER GDNS CT

MANOR RD

ATHERLEY RD

CHARLES CT

GILBERT MEAD

NEWTOWN LA

SYCAMORE DR

FATHOMS

Newtown

Gable Head

ITHICA

BURWOOD GRO

GROVE

DUNDONAL CL

EASTWOOD CL

BEECH GRO

POPLAR

LABURNAM GRO

Tourner Bury Farm

LANE

TOURNER BURY

CHURCH

I S L A N D

HAWTHORNE GRO

South Hayling

LEGION RD

PALMERS TON RD

School

Fire Sta

School Library

Barn Theatre

STATION AVENUE

FURNISS WAY

DANCES WAY

JAMES RD

WEST

DAMFIELD DR

AUBREY

OAKLAND

CAVLAND

NEWTOWN LA

SPINNAKER REACH

LEXDEN GDNS

SOUTHLEIGH GRO

ST MARYS

ROAD

CHERRY WOOD GDS

WALNUT TREE GRO

FIR TREE RD

LINDEN GRO

BROAD WOOD GDS

ST LEONARDS

SPENCER CL

MENGHAM CT

ST MARGARETS RD

GOLDRING

ST LORDS

OSPREY DR

RICHMOND DR

RICHMOND CL

STAUNTON AVENUE

Community Centre

Hayling Park Playing Fields

West Town

West Town

FERNHURST CL

BACON

WINSTON CL

STAMFORD AV

MAGDALA RD

NICHOLAS LANE

GREEN LANE

LENNOX

BEACH ROAD

ST MARYS ROAD

GARDEN CLOSE

HOLLOW

WESTFIELD

Police Sta.

School

OAKWOOD

ELWELL GRN

ELDON GDNS

ASHFORD

ELM

Health Cent

MENGHAM RD

MENGHAM LANE

SELSMORE

ROAD

Mengham

ELM CLOSE ESTATE

P C

SEA FRONT ESTATE

NORMAN

HAROLD

OLD SCHOO

ST ANDREWS ROAD

NORTH CRES

WEST MEAD

WARD

NORFOLK CRES

ANNES

MARK ANTHONY CT

ELDON

WESTFIELD

VICTORIA AV

Westfield

ALEXANDRA AV

TUDOR

CHICHESTER AV

MANOR

SEAGROVE AV

RAMSEY AV

LYNDHURST AV

RITCHIE

WAY

GRAND PAR

THE SANDERLINGS

WEBB CL

ORCHARD RD

WYBORN CL

Amusement Park

SEAFRONT

WEBB

Coastguard Lookout

H a y l i n g

B a y

Hayling Billy Coastal Path

ROAD

i

C

P

CP

CP

CP

P

P

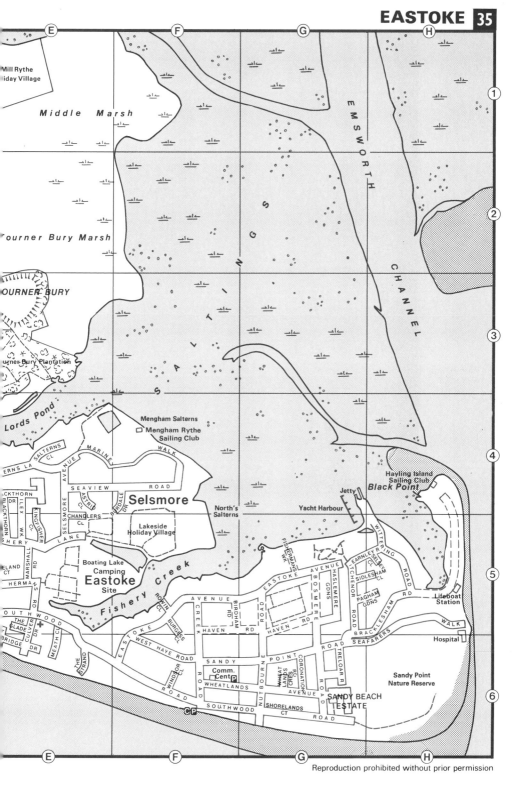

E F G H

① ② ③ ④ ⑤ ⑥

Mill Rythe
iday Village

Middle Marsh

ourner Bury Marsh

OURNER BURY

urner Bury Plantation

E M S W O R T H

S A L T I N G S

C H A N N E L

Lords Pond

Mengham Salterns
☐ Mengham Rythe
Sailing Club

SALTERNS CL

ERNS LA

MARINE

WALK

AVENUE

SEAVIEW

ROAD

Selsmore

North's
Salterns

Hayling Island
Sailing Club
Black Point

Jetty

Yacht Harbour

CKTHORN
DR
ILEX
WK

BLACKTHORN

HERY

KINGFISHER

SELSMORE

LANE

ASTRID

CL

AIRDALE

DR

CHANDLERS
CL

Lakeside
Holiday Village

WITTERING ROAD

FISHERMANS
WK

EARNLEY CL

SIDLESHAM CL

EASTOKE

AVENUE

BOSMERE

HASLEMERE GDNS

TICHENOR

PAGHAM
GDNS

Lifeboat
Station

WALK

Boating Lake
Camping
Eastoke
Site

Fishery Creek

ROWIN
CL

AVENUE

CREEK

BIRDHAM
RD

ROAD

HAVEN

RD

EASTOKE

ROAD

HAVEN

RD

SEAFARERS

BRACKLESHAM

RD

Hospital

ELAND
CT

HERMA

MARSHALL
RD

SOUTHWOOD

CULVER
RD

THE
BLADE

BRIDGE
DR

MEATH CL

THE STRAND

WINDSOR
CL

EASTOKE

ROAD

WEST HAYE ROAD

BURGESS
CL

AVENUE

HAVEN

RD

SANDY

Comm.
Cent

WHEATLANDS

SOUTHWOOD

NUTBOURNE

POINT

WHEAT
LANDS
CRES

SHORELANDS
CT

AVENUE

CORONATION

ROAD

TRELOAR R

SANDY BEACH
ESTATE

Sandy Point
Nature Reserve

CP

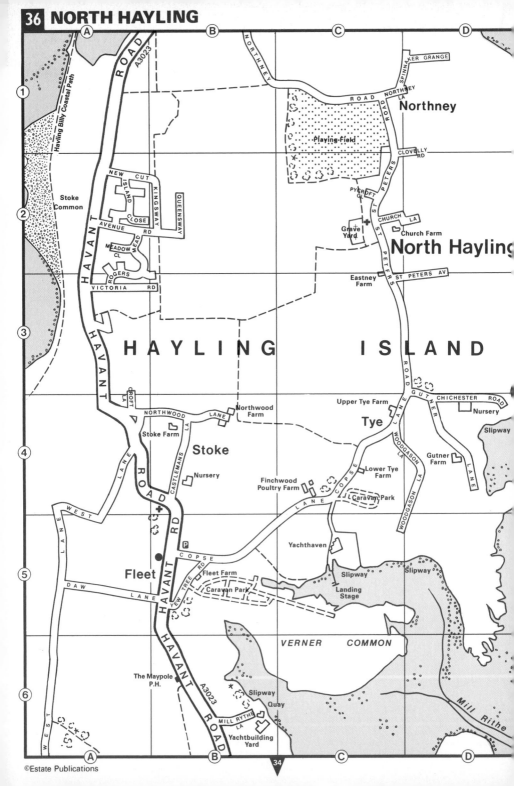

North Hayling

Northney

HAYLING   ISLAND

Tye

Stoke

Fleet

VERNER   COMMON

Spinnaker Grange

Playing-Field

Stoke Common

Church Farm
Grave Yard
Eastney Farm

Upper Tye Farm
Lower Tye Farm
Gutner Farm
Nursery
Slipway

Northwood Farm
Stoke Farm
Nursery

Finchwood Poultry Farm
Caravan Park
Yachthaven

Fleet Farm
Caravan Park
Slipway
Landing Stage
Slipway

The Maypole P.H.
Slipway
Quay
Yachtbuilding Yard

Mill Rithe

Havant Billy Coastal Path

HAVANT ROAD A3023
NORTHNEY ROAD
NEW CUT
ISLAND CLOSE
KINGSWAY RD
QUEENSWAY
AVENUE
MEADOW CL
MEAD
ROGERS
VICTORIA RD

ST PETERS ROAD
CLOVELLY RD
PYCROFT CL
CHURCH LA
ST PETERS AV

NORTHWOOD LANE
CASTLEMANS LA
CROFT LA

WEST LANE
DAW LANE

HAVANT RD
COPSE LANE
YEW TREE RD

GUTNER LANE
WOODGASON LA
CHICHESTER ROAD
ROAD

MILL RYTHE LA
HAVANT ROAD A3023

A - Z INDEX TO STREETS
with Postcodes

The Index includes some names for which there is insufficient space on the maps. These names are preceded by an * and are followed by the nearest adjoining thoroughfare.

37

Cador Dri. PO16 16 A5
Cairo Ter. PO2 26 B3
Caldecote Walk. PO5 6 E4
Calshot Rd. PO9 14 B4
Camber Pl. PO1 29 E5
Camber Quay. PO1 6 A4
Cambridge Junction. PO1 6 C4
Cambridge Rd. PO1 6 C4
Camcross Clo. PO6 17 F3
Camelia Clo. PO9 21 H2
Camelot Cres. PO16 16 A3
Campbell Cres. PO7 12 D6
Campbell Rd. PO5 30 D3
Campion Clo. PO5 13 G5
Canal Walk. PO1 26 A6
Cannock Lawn. PO5 6 F4
Cannons Barn Clo. PO16 16 B3
Canterbury Rd. PO4 31 F3
Capel Ley. PO7 19 G1
*Captains Row,
   White Hart Rd. PO1 29 E5
Carbery Ct. PO9 14 B4
Carberry Dri. PO16 16 B5
Carbis Clo. PO6 17 F4
Cardiff Rd. PO2 24 C6
Cardinal Dri. PO7 13 H2
Carisbrooke Clo. PO9 21 H3
Carisbrooke Rd. PO4 31 G1
Carlisle Rd. PO5 30 D1
Carlton Rd. PO12 28 A3
Carlton Rd. PO16 16 C2
Carlton Way. PO12 28 B3
Carmarthen Av. PO6 19 E4
Carnarvon Rd. PO2 26 D2
Carne Pl. PO6 17 F4
Carpenter Clo. PO4 31 H3
Carronade Walk. PO3 25 E2
Carshalton Av. PO6 19 E5
Cascades App. PO1 6 E1
Cascades Shopping Centre.
   PO1 6 E1
Castle Av. PO9 21 H4
Castle Clo. PO5 30 C3
Castle Esplanade. PO5 30 C6
Castle Gro. PO16 16 C4
Castle Rd. PO5 30 B3
Castle Rd. PO9 15 E1
Castle St. PO16 16 C4
Castle Trading Est. PO16 16 B4
Castle View Rd. PO16 16 C5
Castle Way. PO9 21 H4
Castlemans La. PO11 36 B4
Catherington La. PO8 11 E1
Catherington Way. PO9 21 F1
Catisfield Rd. PO4 31 H1
Causeway Farm. PO8 11 F3
Cavell Dri. PO6 18 B4
Cavendish Clo. PO7 13 G3
Cavendish Dri. PO7 13 G3
Cavendish Rd. PO5 30 C3
Cecil Av. PO5 30 B3
Cecil Pl. PO5 30 B3
Cedar Clo. PO7 13 F5
Cedar Cres. PO8 11 F4
Cedar Gro. PO3 27 F4
Celandine Av. PO8 11 F5
Celia Clo. PO7 13 H3
Cemetery La. PO7 9 B2
Cemetery La. PO10 23 F2
Centaur St. PO2 26 A2
Central Rd. PO6 19 E6
Central Rd. PO16 16 A4
Central St. PO1 26 B5
Chadderton Gdns. PO1 30 A3
Chaffinch Grn. PO8 10 D4
Chalcot Lawn. PO9 14 B5
Chalk Hill Rd. PO8 11 G1
Chalk Pit Rd. PO6 17 F2
Chalk Ridge. PO8 8 C4
Chalkridge Rd. PO6 18 D4
Chalky Wk. PO16 16 B4
Chalton Cres. PO9 20 D1
Chalton La. PO8 8 B1
Chandlers Clo. PO11 35 E5
Chantry Rd. PO8 11 F1
Chapel La. PO7 13 E4
Chapel St. PO2 26 B3
Chapel St. PO5 30 B3
Chaplains Av. PO8 10 B5
Chaplains Clo. PO8 10 B5

*Charlcot Lawn,
   Saxley Ct. PO9 14 B5
Charles Clo. PO7 13 E5
Charles Dickens St. PO1 6 E3
Charles St. PO1 26 B5
Charleston Clo. PO11 34 A3
Charlesworth Av. PO7 13 E1
Charlesworth Dri. PO7 12 D2
Charlesworth Gdns. PO7 13 E2
Charlotte St. PO1 6 E1
Charminster Clo. PO7 13 F3
Chartwell Dri. PO9 22 A3
Chasewater Av. PO3 27 E3
Chatburn Av. PO8 10 D6
Chatham Dri. PO1 30 A3
Chatsworth Av. PO6 25 E1
Chaucer Av. PO6 16 D2
Chaucer Clo. PO7 13 E1
Chedworth Cres. PO6 17 F2
Chelmsford Rd. PO2 25 E5
Chelsea Rd. PO5 30 D3
Cheltenham Rd. PO6 18 A5
Chepstow Ct. PO7 13 H2
Cheriton Clo. PO8 11 E2
Cheriton Clo. PO9 14 B6
Cherry Tree Av. PO8 11 F6
Cherry Wood Gdns. PO11 34 C3
Chervil Clo. PO8 8 C6
Cheshire Way. PO10 23 H4
Cheslyn Rd. PO3 27 F5
Chester Pl. PO5 30 C4
Chesterfield Rd. PO3 27 E2
Chesterton Gdns. PO8 10 C5
Chestnut Av. PO9 20 B2
Chestnut Av. PO8 11 F4
Chestnut Av. PO4 31 F2
Chestnut Clo. PO7 9 B2
Chetwynd Rd. PO4 31 E3
Chevening Ct. PO4 27 G6
Chewter Clo. PO5 30 D5
Chichester Av. PO11 34 C5
Chichester Rd. PO11 36 D4
Chichester Rd. PO2 26 B2
Chidham Clo. PO9 21 E3
Chidham Dri. PO9 21 E3
Chidham Rd. PO6 18 D4
Chidham Sq. PO9 21 E3
Chilbourne Ct. PO9 15 F5
Chilcombe Clo. PO9 21 F2
Chilcote Rd. PO3 27 F4
Childe Sq. PO2 24 B5
Chilgrove Rd. PO6 19 E5
Chilsdown Way. PO7 13 F6
Chilworth Gdns. PO8 8 C3
Chipstead Rd. PO6 18 C5
Chitty Rd. PO4 31 G4
Chivers Clo. PO5 30 C2
Christchurch Gdns. PO7 19 E3
Christopher Way. PO10 22 D3
Church Clo. PO8 8 B1
Church La. PO9 21 H5
Church La. PO11 36 C2
Church Path. PO10 22 A6
Church Path,
   Emsworth. PO10 22 D5
Church Path. PO12 28 C4
Church Path. PO8 11 H3
Church Rd. PO11 34 C3
Church Rd, Landport. PO1 26 B5
Church Rd,
   Portsmouth. PO1 26 B5
Church Rd,
   Southbourne. PO10 23 H6
Church Rd,
   Westbourne. PO10 23 E2
Church St. PO1 26 A4
Church Vw. PO4 31 H1
Church Vw. PO10 23 E2
Churcher Rd. PO10 23 F1
Churchill Ct. PO8 11 E3
Churchill Dri. PO10 22 C2
Cinderford Clo. PO9 17 G2
Circular Rd. PO1 6 D1
Civic Centre Rd. PO9 21 F3
Clacton Rd. PO6 18 A5
Claire Gdns. PO8 8 C5
Claremont Gdns. PO7 19 G1
Claremont Rd. PO1 26 C6
Clarence Esplanade. PO5 30 A4
Clarence Par. PO5 30 B4
Clarence Rd. PO12 28 B3

Clarence Rd. PO5 30 D5
Clarence St. PO1 29 H1
Clarendon Pl, Portsea. PO1 26 B4
Clarendon Pl,
   Portsmouth. PO1 6 F2
Clarendon Rd PO9 21 E4
Clarendon Rd. PO5 30 C4
Clarendon St. PO1 26 B4
Clarkes Rd. PO1 26 D5
Claxton St. PO1 26 B6
Claybank Rd. PO3 25 F6
Claybank Spur. PO3 25 F6
Claydon Av. PO4 31 G1
Cleeve Clo. PO6 17 G3
Clegg Rd. PO4 31 G3
Clement Atlee Way. PO6 17 F4
Cleveland Rd. PO5 31 E2
Clifton Cres. PO7 9 D3
Clifton Rd. PO5 30 B4
Clifton St. PO1 26 C5
Clifton Ter. PO5 30 B4
Clinton Rd. PO7 12 D1
Clive Gro. PO16 16 B5
Clive Rd. PO1 26 C5
Clock St. PO1 6 B2
Clocktower Dri. PO4 31 H4
Closewood Rd. PO7 12 B2
Clovelly Rd. PO10 22 C6
Clovelly Rd. PO11 36 C2
Clovelly Rd. PO4 31 G2
Clovelly Rd. PO10 23 G5
Clover Ct. PO7 13 G5
Clydebank Rd. PO2 26 B2
Coates Way. PO7 13 F6
Cobblewood. PO10 22 C3
Cobden Av. PO3 27 E2
Coburg St. PO1 26 B5
Cockleshell Gdns. PO4 32 A4
Colbury Gro. PO9 14 B6
Colchester Rd. PO6 18 B4
Coldharbour Farm Rd.
   PO10 22 D4
Coldhill La. PO8 10 C2
*Coldon Grn,
   Heckfield Clo. PO9 15 F5
Colebrook Av. PO3 27 F3
Colemore Sq. PO9 21 F1
Coleridge Gdns. PO8 10 D5
Coleridge Rd. PO6 16 D2
Colesbourne Rd. PO6 17 F3
Colinton Av. PO16 16 C3
College Clo. PO9 15 G2
College La. PO1 6 B3
College Rd PO7 19 G4
College Rd. PO1 6 B2
College St. PO1 6 B3
Collington Cres. PO6 17 G3
Collingwood Rd. PO5 30 D4
Collins Rd. PO4 31 G4
Collis Rd. PO3 27 E2
Colpoy St. PO5 6 E4
Coltsfoot Dri. PO7 13 G6
Coltsmead. PO6 17 E4
Colville Rd. PO6 18 D5
Colwell Rd. PO6 18 C6
Comfrey Clo. PO8 8 C6
Comley Hill. PO9 15 H6
Commercial Pl. PO1 6 F1
Commercial Rd. PO1 6 E2
Common St. PO1 26 B5
Commonside. PO10 23 E1
Compass Rd. PO6 17 G4
Compton Clo. PO9 21 F2
Compton Rd. PO2 24 D5
Conan Rd. PO2 24 D4
Conford Ct. PO9 14 B5
Conifer Clo. PO8 11 G4
Conigar Rd. PO10 22 D2
Coniston Av. PO3 27 E2
Connaught La. PO6 16 D3
Connaught Rd. PO9 21 G4
Connaught Rd. PO2 24 C6
Convent La. PO10 22 C5
Cooks La. PO10 23 H5
Coombs Clo. PO8 8 C6
Cooper Gro. PO6 16 C5
Cooper Rd. PO3 27 G3
Copnor Rd. PO3 27 E1
Copper Beech Dri. PO6 19 H5
Copper St. PO5 30 B3
Coppins Gro. PO16 16 B5

Copse Clo. PO7 19 G3
Copse La. PO11 36 B5
Copsey Clo. PO6 19 G5
Copsey Gro. PO6 19 F6
Copythorn Rd. PO2 25 E6
Coral Clo. PO16 16 B5
Coralin Gro. PO7 14 A2
Corbett Rd. PO7 12 E6
Corby Cres. PO3 25 G3
Corhampton Cres. PO9 21 E1
Cornaway La. PO16 16 A4
Cornbrook Gro. PO7 14 A2
Cornelius Dri. PO7 13 H2
Corner Meac. PO7 9 B3
Cornmill. PO1 6 F1
Cornwall Rd. PO1 26 C6
Cornwallis Cres. PO1 26 A4
Coronation Rd. PO11 35 G6
Cosham Park Av. PO6 18 C6
Cotswold Clo. PO9 14 C5
Cottage Clo. PO7 9 B3
Cottage Gro. PO5 6 F4
Cottage Vw. PO1 26 B6
Cotton Dri. PO10 22 C2
Cotwell Av. PO8 11 F5
Court Clo. PO6 18 D6
Court La. PO6 18 D6
Court Mead. PO6 18 D5
Courtland Ter. PO8 11 E5
Courtmount Gro. PO6 18 D5
Courtmount Path. PO6 18 D5
Cousins Gro. PO4 31 G5
Coverack Way. PO6 17 G5
Covert Gro. PO7 13 G6
Covington Rd. PO10 23 E1
Cow La. PO6 18 B6
Cow La. PO16 16 C5
Cowan Rd. PO7 13 E5
Cowper Rd. PO1 26 C4
Crabbe Ct. PO5 6 F4
Crabwood Ct. PO9 14 B4
Craigwell Rd. PO7 19 G1
Cranborne Rd. PO6 18 D4
Cranbourne Rd. PO12 28 A5
Craneswater Av. PO4 31 E5
Craneswater Gate. PO4 31 E5
Craneswater Gdns. PO4 31 F5
Craneswater Park. PO4 31 F4
Cranleigh Av. PO1 26 D4
Cranleigh Rd. PO1 26 D4
Cranleigh Rd. PO16 16 A4
Crasswell St. PO1 6 F1
Crawley Av. PO9 15 E5
Credenhill Rd. PO6 17 H3
Creek End. PO10 22 C6
Creek Rd. PO12 28 B4
Creek Rd. PO11 35 F5
Cressy Rd. P?2 26 B3
Crestland Clo. PO8 11 E6
Cricket Dri. PO8 11 E3
Crinoline Gdns. PO4 31 H4
Crisspyn Clo. PO8 11 F3
Crockford Rd. PO10 23 E2
Croft La. PO11 36 A4
Croft Rd. PO2 26 B1
Crofton Clo. PO7 12 D6
Crofton Rd. PO4 31 H1
Crofton Rd. PO2 24 D5
Cromarty Av. PO4 31 H2
Crombie Clo. PO8 10 D4
Cromer Rd. PO6 18 B4
Cromwell Rd. PO4 31 H4
Crondall Av. PO9 14 D5
Crooked Walk La. PO17 16 D1
Crookham Clo. PO9 20 C1
Crookhorn La. PO7 19 G4
Cross La. PO8 11 E4
Cross St. PO1 6 B2
Cross St. PO5 6 F4
Cross Way. PO9 21 E3
Crossbill Clo. PO8 11 E2
Crossland Clo. PO12 28 A6
Crossland Dri. PO9 21 F2
Crouch La. PO8 11 E1
Crown Clo. PO7 19 G2
Crown St. PO1 26 B5
Crowsbury Clo. PO10 22 C2
Crystal Way. PO7 13 H3
Culver Dri. PO11 35 E5
Culver Rd. PO4 31 G5
Culverin Sq. PO3 25 E3

Fitzherbert Spur. PO6	19 G6	Galaxie Rd. PO8	11 E5
Fitzherbert St. PO1	29 H1	Galt Rd. PO6	19 G5
Fitzpatrick Ct. PO6	18 A4	Gamble Rd. PO2	26 B2
Fitzroy Walk. PO1	26 B5	Garden Clo. PO11	34 B4
Fitzwygram Cres. PO9	21 F2	Garden Ct. PO16	16 C4
Five Heads Rd. PO8	11 F1	Garden La. PO5	30 B3
Flag Walk. PO8	10 D4	Garden Ter. PO5	30 D4
Flathouse Rd. PO1	29 H1	Garfield Rd. PO2	26 A2
Fleetend Clo. PO9	14 C5	Garland Av. PO10	22 D3
Flexford Gdns. PO9	21 G2	Garnier St. PO1	26 B6
Flint St. PO5	30 B3	Garsons Rd. PO10	23 G5
Florence Rd. PO5	30 D5	Gatcombe Av. PO3	25 E5
Florentine Way. PO7	13 H3	Gatcombe Dri. PO2	24 D4
Flying Bull Clo. PO2	26 B2	Gatehouse Rd. PO16	16 A5
Flying Bull La. PO2	26 B2	Gaulter Clo. PO9	21 G2
Folkestone Rd. PO3	27 E3	Geoffrey Av. PO7	19 E3
Fontwell Mews. PO7	14 A2	George Byng Way. PO1	26 A2
Fontwell Rd. PO5	30 C4	George St PO12	28 A3
Fordingbridge Rd. PO4	32 A4	George St. PO1	26 C3
Foreland Ct. PO11	35 E5	Gibraltar Rd. PO4	32 B4
Forest Av. PO8	11 E5	Gilbert Mead. PO11	34 B3
Forest Clo. PO8	10 D5	Gilbert Way. PO7	13 F6
Forest End. PO7	13 E4	Gillman Rd. PO6	19 H4
Forest Mead. PO7	9 B4	Gitsham Gdns. PO7	19 F2
Forest Rd. PO7	9 A3	Gladstone Gdns. PO16	16 B5
Forestside Av. PO9	15 F5	Gladstone Pl. PO2	26 B2
Forsythia Clo. PO9	21 H1	Gladys Av. PO8	11 E5
Fort Cumberland Rd. PO4	32 B4	Gladys Av. PO2	24 C5
Forton Av. PO12	28 A3	Glamis Clo. PO7	13 G3
Forton Rd. PO1	26 C5	Glamorgan Rd. PO8	8 B5
Fortunes Way. PO9	20 A4	Glasgow Rd. PO4	32 A4
Foster Rd. PO1	26 B4	Glasspool. PO7	9 A2
Fountain St. PO1	6 E2	Glebe Clo. PO11	34 A2
*Four Marks Grn,		Glebe Park Av. PO9	20 B4
Wyeford Clo. PO9	15 G5	Glebefield Gdns. PO6	18 B5
Fourth Av. PO6	18 B5	Glencoe Rd. PO1	26 D3
Fourth Av. PO9	21 H3	Glendale. PO9	15 G2
Fourth St. PO1	26 D4	Gleneagles Dri. PO7	14 A1
Foxbury Gro. PO16	16 A5	Glenleigh Av. PO6	18 C6
Foxbury La. PO10	23 F2	Glenleigh Pk. PO9	21 H3
Foxcott Gro. PO9	14 D6	Glenthorne Rd. PO3	25 F6
Foxes Clo. PO7	13 E5	Glenwood Gdns. PO8	10 D6
Foxley Dri. PO3	25 G3	Glenwood Rd. PO10	23 H4
Frances Rd. PO7	19 F2	Glidden Clo. PO1	26 B6
Francis Av. PO4	31 F4	Gloucester Mews. PO5	30 C2
Francis Rd. PO8	8 C4	Gloucester Pl. PO5	30 C3
Frankland Ter. PO10	22 D6	Gloucester Rd. PO1	6 B1
Frarydene. PO10	23 G6	Gloucester Rd. PO7	13 F5
Fraser Gdns. PO10	23 H4	Gloucester Ter. PO5	30 B2
Fraser Rd. PO9	20 D3	Gloucester Vw. PO5	30 C2
Fraser Rd. PO2	24 A6	Godiva Lawn. PO4	32 B4
Fraser Rd. PO5	30 D2	Godwin Clo. PO10	22 C2
Fratton Ind Est. PO3	27 E6	Godwin Cres. PO8	8 C3
Fratton Rd. PO1	26 C4	Godwit Rd. PO4	27 G5
Frederick St. PO1	29 H1	Gofton Av. PO6	19 E6
*Freefolk Grn,		Gold St. PO5	30 B3
Warbrook Ct. PO9	15 F5	Goldcrest Clo. PO8	11 E2
Freestone Rd. PO5	30 C4	Goldring Clo. PO11	34 C4
French St. PO1	29 F5	Goldsmith Av. PO4	31 E1
Frenchies View. PO7	9 A2	Goodwood Clo. PO8	13 H2
Frendstaple Rd. PO7	13 G6	Goodwood Clo. PO10	23 H6
Frensham Rd. PO4	31 F2	Goodwood Rd. PO5	30 D4
Freshfield Gdns. PO7	13 F3	Gordon Rd. PO10	23 E6
Freshwater Rd. PO6	18 B6	Gordon Rd. PO1	30 A3
Friary Clo. PO5	30 C4	Gordon Rd. PO7	13 E5
Frobisher Gro. PO16	16 B4	Goring Av. PO8	8 C3
Froddington Rd. PO5	30 D1	Gorley Ct. PO9	14 B5
Frogham Grn. PO9	14 B5	Gorseway. PO11	33 H4
Frogmore La. PO8	10 D4	Grafton St. PO2	26 A3
Frogmore Rd. PO4	31 G1	Graham Rd. PO4	31 E3
Froxfield Gdns. PO16	16 C2	Granada Clo. PO8	11 E5
Froxfield Rd. PO9	15 F6	Granada Rd. PO4	31 E5
Froyle Ct. PO9	15 F6	Grand Par. PO11	34 C5
Fulflood Rd. PO9	14 C6	Grand Par. PO1	29 F5
Fullerton Clo. PO9	15 F5	Grange Clo. PO8	21 G3
Fulmer Walk. PO8	10 C4	Grange Rd. PO2	24 C6
Funtington Rd. PO2	26 D2	Grant Rd. PO6	19 G5
Furdies. PO7	9 A3	Granville Clo. PO9	21 G4
Furness Rd. PO5	30 D6	Grassmere Way. PO7	14 A2
Furniss Way. PO11	34 A3	Grateley Cres. PO9	20 C1
Furnston Gro. PO10	23 H4	Grayland Clo. PO11	34 A3
Furze La. PO4	27 H6	Grays Ct. PO1	6 C4
Furze Way. PO6	11 F4	Grayshott Rd. PO4	31 F2
Furzedown Cres. PO9	15 E6	Great Copse Dri. PO9	14 C5
Furzeley Ct. PO9	14 B5	Great Mead. PO7	9 C4
Furzeley Rd. PO7	9 B4	Great Southsea St. PO5	30 B3
Fuschia Clo. PO9	22 A2	Greatfield Way. PO9	9 B6
Fyning St. PO1	26 B5	Grebe Clo. PO8	10 C5
		Green Farm Gdns. PO3	25 E4
Gains Rd. PO4	31 E4	Green La. PO8	8 A1

Green La. Clanfield. PO8	8 C2	Harold Rd. PO11	34 D5
Green La. PO7	9 A2	Harold Rd. PO4	31 E3
Green La. PO11	34 A4	Harold Rd. PO10	23 E2
Green La. PO3	25 E5	Harrier Clo. PO8	11 E2
Green Rd. PO5	6 F4	Harrow Rd. PO5	31 E2
Greenacre Gdns. PO7	19 F2	Hart Plain Av,	
Greenfield Court. PO10	22 D2	Waterlooville. PO8	13 F1
Greenfield Cres. PO8	11 F4	Hart Plain Av,	
Greenfield Rise. PO8	11 F6	Wecock. PO8	10 C5
Greenlea Clo. PO7	19 E3	Harting Clo. PO8	8 C3
Greenwood Av. PO6	18 A5	Harting Gdns. PO16	16 B2
Greetham St. PO5	6 F3	Hartland Ct. PO10	23 G5
Grenville Rd. PO4	31 E2	Hartley Rd. PO2	24 C5
Greville Grn. PO10	22 C2	Harts Farm Clo. PO9	20 D5
Greywell Precinct. PO9	14 D6	Harts Farm Way. PO9	20 C5
Greywell Rd. PO9	14 D6	Hartwell Rd. PO3	25 G4
Grindle Clo. PO16	16 B2	Hartwood Gdns. PO8	13 F1
Gritanwood Rd. PO4	32 A4	*Harvest Gate Walk,	
Grosvenor St. PO5	6 F4	Woolston Rd. PO9	14 B5
Grove Av. PO12	28 A3	Harvest Rd. PO7	9 A2
Grove Av. PO16	16 B6	Harvey Rd. PO6	18 B4
Grove Buildings. PO12	28 A4	Harwich Rd. PO6	18 A4
Grove Rd, Cosham. PO6	19 E6	Haslar Bri. PO12	28 B4
Grove Rd, Havant. PO9	21 F4	Haslar Cres. PO7	12 D1
Grove Rd North. PO5	30 C3	Haslar Rd. PO12	28 B6
Grove Rd South. PO5	30 C4	Haslemere Gdns. PO11	35 G5
Gruneisen Rd. PO2	24 B5	Haslemere Rd. PO4	31 F4
Guardhouse Rd. PO1	29 G1	Haslemere Rd. PO10	23 G4
Guardroom Rd. PO24	24 A6	Hatch Ct. PO9	14 B4
Guildford Clo. PO10	23 H5	Hatfield Rd. PO4	31 G3
Guildford Rd. PO1	26 C5	Hathaway Gdns. PO7	13 H2
Guildhall Sq. PO1	29 H3	Hatherley Cres. PO16	16 A4
Guildhall Walk. PO1	6 E3	Hatherley Dri. PO16	16 A4
Gun Wharf Rd. PO1	6 B4	Hatherley Rd. PO6	17 F3
Gunners Row. PO4	31 H4	Havant Business Centre.	
Gunstore Rd. PO3	25 E3	PO9	20 D5
Gurnard Rd. PO6	18 B6	Havant By-Pass. PO9	20 D4
Gurney Rd. PO4	32 A3	Havant Farm Clo. PO9	21 F2
Gutner La. PO11	36 D4	Havant Rd. PO6	18 C5
Gwatkin Clo. PO9	20 C2	Havant Rd. PO10	22 A5
Gypsy La. PO8	10 D4	Havant Rd. PO8	11 H2
		Havant Rd. PO11	36 A3
Hadleigh Rd. PO6	18 A5	Havant Rd. PO2	26 B1
Hale St North. PO1	26 B4	Havant St. PO1	6 B2
Hale St South. PO1	26 B5	Havelock Rd. PO5	30 D2
Half Moon St. PO1	6 B2	Haven Rd. PO11	35 F5
Halfpenny Dell. PO7	19 H2	Havisham Rd. PO2	26 A3
Halfpenny La. PO1	30 A3	Hawke St. PO1	6 B2
Halifax Rise. PO7	13 G4	Hawkewood Av. PO7	10 B6
Hallett Rd. PO9	21 H3	Hawkley Clo. PO9	14 D5
Halliday Cres. PO4	32 B4	*Hawstead Grn,	
Halstead Rd. PO6	18 A5	Mewsey Ct. PO9	14 C4
Ham La. PO8	11 E1	Hawthorn Clo. PO16	16 B3
Ham La. PO10	23 G6	Hawthorn Cres. PO6	25 E1
Hamble La. PO7	13 E6	Hawthorn Rd,	
Hambledon Par. PO7	12 D1	Clanfield. PO8	8 C5
Hambledon Rd,		Hawthorn Rd,	
Denmead. PO7	9 A1	Denmead. PO8	9 A2
Hambledon Rd,		Hawthorne Gro. PO11	34 D3
Waterlooville. PO7	12 C1	Hay St. PO1	6 C2
Hambrook St. PO5	30 B3	Haydock Mews. PO7	13 H2
Hamfield Dri. PO11	34 A3	Hayling Av. PO3	27 E4
Hamilton Clo. PO9	21 F5	Hazel Gro. PO8	8 C2
Hamilton Rd. PO5	30 D4	Hazel Rd. PO8	8 C2
Hamilton Rd. PO16	16 D4	Hazeldean Dri. PO9	15 F2
Hampshire St. PO1	26 C4	Hazelholt Dri. PO9	20 D2
Hampshire Ter. PO1	6 D4	Hazelwood Av. PO9	20 B2
Hampton Clo. PO7	13 G4	Hazely Gdns. PO9	15 F6
Hannah Gdns. PO7	13 F3	Hazleton Ind Est. PO8	11 G3
Hannington Rd. PO9	14 C4	Hazleton Way. PO8	11 F3
Hanover Ct. PO1	29 F5	Heath Clo. PO8	11 F2
Hanover St. PO1	6 B2	Heathcote Rd. PO2	25 E6
Hanway Rd. PO1	26 B3	Heather Clo. PO7	13 G5
Harbour Clo. PO12	28 C3	Heatherton Mews. PO10	22 C3
Harbour Rd. PO11	33 G3	Heathfield Rd. PO2	26 B2
Harbour Tower. PO12	28 C4	Hector Clo. PO7	19 H3
Harbour Vw. PO16	16 B5	*Hedge End Walk,	
*Harbour Walk,		Soldridge Clo. PO9	15 G5
Broad St. PO1	29 E5	Hedgerow Gdns. PO10	22 C2
Harbour Way. PO10	22 D6	Heidelberg Rd. PO4	31 F2
Harbour Way. PO2	24 B5	Helena Rd. PO4	31 F5
Harbridge Ct. PO9	14 C4	Hellyer Rd. PO4	31 G4
Harcourt Clo. PO8	11 E5	Helston Clo. PO10	22 C3
Harcourt Rd. PO4	31 E5	Helston Rd. PO6	17 E3
Hardy Rd. PO6	19 H6	Hemlock Rd. PO8	10 C5
Harestock Rd. PO9	21 E2	Hempsted Rd. PO6	17 G3
Harkness Dri. PO7	14 A3	Hemsley Walk. PO8	11 E5
Harleston Rd. PO6	18 A4	Henderson Rd. PO4	32 A4
Harley Walk. PO1	26 B5	Henley Rd. PO4	31 F4
		Henry St. PO12	28 B4

41

Herbert Rd. PO4	31 E4	Holt Gdns. PO9	9 B5

Herbert Rd. PO4 31 E4
Herbert St. PO1 26 A3
Hercules St. PO2 26 B2
Hereford Rd. PO5 30 D3
Hermitage Clo. PO9 21 E1
Hermitage Gdns. PO7 13 G3
Herne Rd. PO6 18 B5
Heron Clo. PO4 27 F6
Heron Quay. PO10 23 E6
Herriot Clo. PO8 11 E4
Hertford Pl. PO1 26 B4
Hester Rd. PO4 32 A3
Hewett Rd. PO2 24 D5
Heyshott Gdns. PO8 8 C3
Heyshott Rd. PO4 31 F2
Heyward Rd. PO4 31 E2
Heywood Gdns. PO9 14 B5
High Lawn Way. PO9 14 D6
High St, Cosham. PO6 18 C6
High St, Emsworth. PO10 22 D5
High St, Gosport. PO12 28 C4
High St, Portsmouth. PO1 29 E5
High Trees. PO7 13 F3
High View. PO16 16 B2
Highbank Av. PO7 19 E2
Highbury Gro. PO6 25 E1
Highbury St. PO1 30 A2
Highbury Way. PO6 25 E1
Highclere Av. PO9 21 E1
Highcroft La. PO8 11 G1
Highfield Av. PO7 13 F2
Highfield Clo. PO7 13 G2
Highfield Par. PO7 13 G2
Highfield Rd. PO1 26 B6
Highgate Rd. PO3 25 E6
Highgrove Ind Pk. PO3 25 F4
Highgrove Rd. PO3 27 F3
Highland Clo. PO10 22 C5
Highland Rd. PO10 22 C5
Highland Rd. PO4 31 F4
Highland St. PO4 31 G4
Highland Ter. PO4 31 F4
Highlands Rd. PO6 19 F5
Highwood Lawn. PO9 14 B4
Higworth La. PO11 34 B2
Hilary Av. PO6 18 D6
Hilda Gdns. PO7 9 C3
Hill Downs Av. PO2 24 B5
Hill Rd. PO16 16 B2
Hill View Rd. PO16 16 B3
Hillborough Cres. PO5 30 D4
Hillbrow Clo. PO9 15 F2
Hillmead Gdns. PO9 20 B3
Hillside Av. PO7 19 E3
Hillside Clo. PO8 8 C4
Hillside Cres. PO6 16 D3
Hillsley Rd. PO6 17 E2
Hilltop Cres. PO6 19 E3
Hilltop Gdns. PO8 8 C4
Hillview. PO8 11 G4
Hilsea Cres. PO2 24 D3
Hiltingbury Rd. PO9 15 E6
Hilton Rd. PO12 28 A5
Hinton Clo. PO9 20 D1
Hinton Daubnay Rd. PO8 8 A4
Hinton Manor La. PO8 8 C3
Hipley Rd. PO9 21 G2
Hither Grn. PO10 23 H3
Hitherwood Clo. PO7 14 A2
Hobbs Pass. PO12 28 C4
Hobby Clo. PO3 25 E3
Hockham Ct. PO9 14 B4
Hockley Clo. PO6 18 B5
Hodges Clo. PO9 21 G2
Holbeach Clo. PO6 18 B4
Holbrook Rd. PO1 26 B5
Holbury Ct. PO9 15 F5
Holcot La. PO3 25 G3
Holdenhurst Clo. PO8 8 C6
Hollam Rd. PO4 31 H1
Holland Rd. PO4 31 E2
Hollow La. PO11 34 B4
Holly Dri. PO7 13 G5
Holly St. PO12 28 A4
Hollybank Clo. PO8 11 G4
Hollybank La. PO10 22 C1
Hollywell Dri. PO6 17 F5
Holman Clo. PO8 13 H1
Holne Ct. PO4 32 B4
Holt Way. PO7 13 F6

Holt Gdns. PO9 9 B5
Holybourne Rd. PO9 21 F2
Holyrood Clo. PO7 13 G4
Home Mead. PO7 9 B3
Homefield Path. PO6 19 F6
Homefield Rd. PO6 19 F6
Homefield Rd. PO10 23 F2
Homefield Way. PO8 8 B1
Homer Clo. PO8 13 F1
Homewell. PO9 21 F4
Honeysuckle Ct. PO7 13 G5
Honeywood Clo. PO3 25 E4
Hooks Farm Way. PO9 20 D2
Hooks La. PO9 20 D2
Hope St. PO1 6 E1
Hopfield Clo. PO7 13 F4
Hopfield Mews. PO7 13 F4
Hopkins Clo. PO6 16 D4
Hordle Rd. PO9 20 C1
Hornbeam Rd. PO9 21 H2
Horndean Rd. PO10 22 B1
Hornet Clo. PO12 28 A5
Horsea La. PO2 24 C3
Horsea Rd. PO2 24 D3
Hospital La. PO16 16 D6
Horsebridge Rd. PO9 21 G1
Houghton Clo. PO9 15 F5
Howard Rd. PO2 24 D3
Hoylake Rd. PO6 19 F4
Hudson Rd. PO5 30 C2
Hulbert Rd. PO9 20 B1
Hulbert Rd PO7 13 F3
Hunter Clo. PO9 31 G3
Hunter Rd. PO6 18 C4
Hunters Ride. PO7 13 E4
Huntley Clo. PO6 17 G3
Hurn Ct. PO9 15 F5
Hursley Rd. PO9 14 C6
Hurst Green Clo. PO8 11 F6
Hurstbourne Clo. PO9 14 C5
Hurstville Dri. PO7 13 F5
Hurstwood Av. PO10 23 H5
Hussar Ct. PO7 12 D2
Hyde Park Rd. PO5 6 F3
Hyde St. PO5 30 B2
Hythe Rd. PO6 18 B5
Ibsley Gro. PO9 20 D2
Icarus Pl. PO7 19 H3
Idsworth Clo. PO8 11 H3
Idsworth Rd. PO7 14 A1
Idsworth Rd. PO3 27 F2
Ilex Walk. PO11 35 E4
Ilford Ct. PO9 15 F5
INDUSTRIAL ESTATES:
Acorn Business Centre. PO6 17 H4
Bilton Business Pk. PO3 25 G5
Castle Trading Est. PO16 16 D4
Eastern Ind Centre. PO6 25 H1
Fairway Business Pk. PO3 25 G5
Fratton Ind Est. PO3 27 E6
Havant Business Centre. PO9 20 D5
Hazleton Ind Est. PO8 11 G3
Highgrove Ind Pk. PO3 25 F4
Kingscroft Ct Ind Est. PO9 20 D4
O'Jays Ind Pk. PO3 25 F6
Parklands Business Pk. PO7 9 A4
Pipers Wood Ind Est. PO7 12 D3
Pyramid Centre. PO3 25 G5
Railway Triangle Ind Est. PO6 25 G1
Shawcross Ind Pk. PO3 25 F2
The Admiral Pk. PO3 25 F4
The Tanneries Ind Est. PO9 21 E4
The Warrior Business Centre. PO6 19 G6
Victory Trading Est. PO3 25 F5
Wessex Gate Ind Est. PO8 11 G3
West Leigh Ind Est. PO9 21 H1
Ingledene Clo. PO9 20 D3
Inglis Rd. PO5 31 E3
Inhurst Av. PO7 13 G3
Inhurst Rd. PO2 24 D5
Inkpen Walk. PO9 14 C4

Inner-by-Pass. PO10 22 D5
Invergordon Av. PO6 19 E6
Inverness Rd. PO1 26 C3
Iping Av. PO9 14 C6
Ireland Way. PO7 13 F6
Ironbridge La. PO4 32 A3
Isambard Brunel Rd. PO1 6 E2
Island Clo. PO11 36 A2
Island View Wk. PO16 16 B2
Islay Gdns. PO6 18 C4
Itchen Rd. PO9 15 G5
Itchenor Rd. PO11 35 G5
Ithica Clo. PO11 34 C3
Ivy Ct. PO7 19 G1
Ivy Lane. PO1 6 B1
Ivy Orchard. PO8 8 B1
Ivydene Gdns. PO8 11 E5
Jack Cockerill. PO5 30 D6
Jackdaw Clo. PO8 10 C5
Jackson Clo. PO6 25 H1
Jacobs Clo. PO8 8 C2
Jacobs St. PO1 6 F1
Jago Rd. PO9 6 A1
Jamaica Pl. PO12 28 A4
James Clo. PO11 34 A3
James Callaghan Way. PO17 16 D1
James Copse Rd. PO8 10 D4
James Howell Ct. PO7 9 B3
James Rd. PO9 21 E3
Japonica Way. PO9 22 A1
Jaqueline Av. PO7 19 G1
Jarndyce Walk. PO2 26 A3
Jasmine Gro. PO7 13 G5
Jasmine Way. PO8 8 C2
Jasmond Rd. PO6 25 E1
Jason Pl. PO7 19 H3
Jay Clo. PO8 11 E2
Jenkins Gro. PO3 27 G4
Jenner Rd. PO6 18 B4
Jersey Rd. PO2 26 C2
Jervis Rd. PO2 24 B5
Jessica Clo. PO7 13 H2
Jessie Clo. PO9 20 C2
Jessie Rd. PO4 31 E2
Jodrell Clo. PO8 11 G2
John King Shipyard. PO10 22 D6
Joseph St. PO12 28 A4
Jubilee Av. PO6 16 D3
Jubilee Rd. PO16 16 C4
Jubilee Rd. PO4 31 F3
Jubilee Rd. PO7 13 E2
Jubilee Ter. PO5 30 B3
Juliet Ct. PO7 13 H3
Juniper Rd. PO8 8 C6
Juniper Sq. PO9 21 F5
Jura Clo. PO6 18 C4
Karen Av. PO6 25 G1
Kassassin St. PO4 31 H4
Kassel Clo. PO7 14 A3
Katrina Gdns. PO11 34 C2
Kearsney Av. PO2 24 D5
Keats Av. PO6 16 D2
Keats Clo. PO8 10 D5
Keel Clo. PO3 25 G4
Kefford Clo. PO8 11 F3
Kelly Rd. PO7 13 F5
Kelsall Av. PO10 23 H4
Kelsey Head. PO6 17 F4
Kelvin Gro. PO16 16 C3
Kempton Pk. PO7 14 A2
Kemshott Ct. PO9 14 B5
Ken Berry Ct. PO9 15 F5
Kendal Av. PO3 27 E1
Kendal Clo. PO8 11 E5
Kenilworth Rd. PO5 30 D5
Kennedy Clo. PO7 19 G1
Kensington Rd. PO12 28 A5
Kensington Rd. PO2 25 E5
Kent Gro. PO6 16 B5
Kent Rd. PO5 30 B3
Kent St. PO1 6 C3
Kentidge Rd. PO7 13 E6
Kenwood Rd. PO16 16 C6
Kenya Rd. PO16 16 A4
Kenyon Rd. PO2 25 E5
Kestrel Clo. PO8 8 C3
Kestrel Pl. PO6 19 H6

Keswick Av. PO3 27 E2
Kettering Ter. PO2 26 A3
Keydell Av. PO8 11 E4
Keydell Clo. PO8 11 E4
Keyhaven Dri. PO9 14 B6
Khandala Gdns. PO7 19 H1
Kidmore La. PO7 9 B1
Kilbride Path. PO2 26 B2
Kilmeston Clo. PO9 14 D5
Kilmeston Clo. PO1 26 C4
Kilmiston Dri. PO16 16 B2
Kiln Rd. PO3 27 F1
Kiln Side. PO7 9 B4
Kilpatrick Clo. PO2 26 B2
Kilwich Way. PO16 16 A6
Kimberley Rd. PO4 31 G4
Kimbolton Rd. PO3 27 E5
Kimbridge Cres. PO9 15 E5
Kimton Ct. PO9 15 F5
King Albert St. PO1 26 B5
King Arthurs Ct. PO6 19 G5
King Charles St. PO1 29 F5
*King Edward Ct, White Hart La. PO1 29 E5
King Edwards Cres. PO2 24 C5
King George Rd. PO16 16 C4
King Henry I St. PO1 6 D3
King John Av. PO16 16 A4
King Richard Clo. PO6 18 A5
King Richard I St. PO1 6 D3
King St, Emsworth. PO10 22 D6
King St. PO12 28 B3
King St. PO5 6 E4
King St, Southbourne. PO10 23 E2
King William St. PO1 6 C1
Kingfisher Clo. PO8 10 C5
Kingfisher Clo. PO9 15 F2
Kingfisher Clo. PO11 35 E5
Kings Bench Alley. PO1 6 C2
Kings Clo. PO9 15 E1
Kings Mede. PO8 11 E3
Kings Rd. PO8 10 D6
Kings Rd. PO10 22 C6
Kings Rd. PO12 28 A3
Kings Rd. PO11 34 C1
Kings Rd. PO1 6 C1
Kings Rd. PO5 30 B2
Kings Ter. PO10 22 D5
Kings Ter. PO5 30 B3
Kingsclere Av. PO9 14 C6
Kingscote Rd. PO6 17 E2
Kingscote Rd. PO8 10 B6
Kingscroft Ct Ind Est. PO9 20 D4
Kingscroft La. PO9 20 D4
Kingsdown Pl. PO1 31 E1
Kingsdown Rd. PO7 12 D1
Kingsland Clo. PO6 17 H3
Kingsley Av. PO10 22 C5
Kingsley Grn. PO9 14 C5
Kingsley Rd. PO4 32 A3
Kingston Cres. PO2 26 B2
Kingston Rd. PO1 26 B2
Kingsway. PO11 36 B2
Kingswell St. PO1 6 E2
Kingsworthy Rd. PO9 21 F2
Kinnell Clo. PO10 22 C5
Kinross Cres. PO6 19 E6
Kintyre Rd. PO6 18 C4
Kipling Rd. PO2 24 D4
Kirby Rd. PO2 24 D6
Kirkstall Rd. PO4 30 D6
Kirtley Clo. PO6 25 G1
Kirton Rd. PO6 19 E6
Kite Clo. PO8 10 C5
*Kitwood Grn, Ropley Rd. PO9 15 F6
Knightwood Av. PO9 15 E6
Knowsley Cres. PO6 18 D6
Knowsley Rd. PO6 18 C6
Knox Clo. PO9 20 D4
Knox Rd. PO2 24 B6
Laburnam Gro. PO11 34 D3
Laburnum Av. PO6 19 F6
Laburnum Gro. PO2 24 C6
Laburnum Gro. PO7 13 E5
Ladies Mile. PO5 30 C5
Ladybridge Rd. PO7 19 F1
Lake End Dri. PO10 22 C5

Lake Rd. PO1 6 F1
Lakeside Av. PO3 27 F4
Lakesmere Rd. PO8 11 G3
Lambert Clo. PO7 13 F6
Lampeter Av. PO6 19 E5
Lancaster Clo. PO16 16 A2
Lancaster Way. PO7 13 F5
Landguard Rd. PO4 31 G3
Landport St. PO1 26 B5
Landport St. PO5 6 D4
Landport Ter. PO5 6 D4
Landport Vw. PO1 6 F1
Langbrook Clo. PO9 21 F5
Langdale Av. PO6 18 D6
Langford Rd. PO1 26 D3
Langley Rd. PO2 26 C2
Langrish Clo. PO9 15 E5
Langstone Av. PO9 21 F6
Langstone Rd. PO9 21 F5
Langstone Rd. PO3 27 E5
Lansdown Av. PO16 16 C6
Lansdowne Av. PO7 19 E3
Lansdowne St. PO5 6 D4
Lantana Clo. PO7 13 G5
Lapwing Clo. PO8 11 E2
Larchfield Way. PO8 11 F4
Larchwood Av. PO9 20 B1
Larkhill Rd. PO3 25 E4
*Larkwhistle Walk,
  Berrydown Rd. PO9 14 B4
*Lasham Gdns,
  Tunworth Ct. PO9 15 F6
*Lasham Grn,
  Newnham Ct. PO9 15 F6
Latchmore Forest Gro. PO8 11 G4
Latchmore Gdns. PO8 10 D6
Latimer Ct. PO3 25 G4
Lauder Clo. PO10 23 H4
Laurel Rd. PO8 11 G4
Laurence Grn. PO10 22 D2
Laurus Clo. PO7 13 G6
Lavant Clo. PO8 13 H2
Lavant Dri. PO9 21 G2
Lavender Rd. PO7 13 G5
Laverock Lea. PO16 16 B3
Lawnswood Clo. PO8 13 G1
Lawrence Av. PO8 10 C6
Lawrence Rd. PO5 31 E4
Lawson Rd. PO5 31 E2
Lazy Acre. PO10 23 G5
Lealand Gro. PO6 19 F5
Lealand Rd. PO6 19 F6
Leckford Clo. PO16 16 B2
Leckford Rd. PO9 15 F5
Ledbury Rd. PO6 17 G3
Legion Rd. PO11 34 C3
Leigh Rd. PO9 21 F3
Leith Av. PO16 16 C3
Lendorber Av. PO6 18 D5
Lennox Lodge. PO11 34 A4
Lennox Rd North. PO5 30 C4
Lennox Rd South. PO5 30 C5
Lennox Row. PO1 6 C1
Lensyd Gdns. PO8 10 D3
Leofric Ct. PO4 32 B4
Leominster Rd. PO6 17 F2
Leonard Rd. PO12 28 A3
Leopold St. PO4 31 E4
Lester Av. PO9 20 D3
Leventhorpe Ct. PO12 28 A4
Lewis Rd. PO10 22 D2
Lexden Gdns. PO11 34 B3
Leyland Clo. PO12 28 A5
Liam Clo. PO9 21 G1
Lichfield Rd. PO3 27 E5
Liddiards Way. PO7 19 H2
Lidiard Gdns. PO4 32 A5
Lightfoot Lawn. PO4 32 B4
Lilac Clo. PO9 22 A2
Lily Av. PO7 19 E3
Limberline Rd. PO3 25 E3
Limberline Spur. PO3 25 E3
Lime Gro. PO6 17 F2
Lime Gro. PO11 33 G3
Lincoln Rise. PO8 11 E5
Lincoln Road. PO1 26 C6
Lind Clo. PO7 19 H2
Linda Gro. PO8 10 D6
Linden Clo. PO10 22 C3
Linden Gro. PO11 34 C3

Linden Lea. PO16 16 B3
Linden Way. PO9 21 F2
Linden Way. PO8 11 F3
Lindisfarne Clo. PO6 18 D5
Lindley Av. PO4 31 G4
Linford Ct. PO9 14 B4
Link Rd. PO9 20 D1
Linkenholt Way. PO9 20 C1
Linklater Path. PO1 26 B4
Links Clo. PO9 15 F1
Links La. PO9 15 F1
Links Rd. PO11 33 G4
Linnet Clo. PO8 10 C4
Lion St. PO1 6 C2
Lion Ter. PO1 6 D2
Lisle Way. PO10 22 C2
Liss Rd. PO4 31 F2
Lister Rd. PO6 18 B5
Lith Cres. PO8 8 B6
Lith La. PO8 8 B6
Little Arthur St. PO2 26 C3
Little Britain St. PO1 6 C3
Little Coburg St. PO1 26 B5
Little Corner. PO7 9 B4
Little George St. PO1 26 C3
Little Hyden La. PO8 8 B1
Little Mead. PO7 9 C4
Little Southsea St. PO5 30 B3
Littlegreen Av. PO9 21 G2
Littlepark Av. PO9 20 B2
Littleton Gro. PO9 21 F1
Liverpool Rd. PO1 26 C5
Livesay Gdns. PO3 27 E5
Livingstone Rd. PO5 30 D3
Lobelia Ct. PO7 13 G5
Locarno Rd. PO3 25 E5
Lock App. PO6 17 F5
Lock Vw. PO6 17 F4
Lockerley Rd. PO9 21 G2
Locksheath Clo. PO9 14 B5
Locksway Rd. PO4 31 H2
Lodge Av. PO6 18 D5
Lodge Rd. PO9 20 C4
Lodgebury Clo. PO10 23 H5
Lodsworth Clo. PO8 8 C3
Lombard St. PO1 29 F5
Lombardy Rise. PO7 13 G6
Lomond Clo. PO2 26 B2
Londesborough Rd. PO4 31 E3
London Av. PO2 24 C5
London Rd, Clanfield. PO8 8 C6
London Rd. PO6 18 C5
London Rd.
  Horndean. PO8 11 H2
London Rd. PO2 26 B2
Lone Valley. PO7 19 F2
Long Acre Ct. PO1 26 C4
Long Copse La. PO10 22 C1
Long Curtain Rd. PO1 30 A4
Longdean Clo. PO6 17 E2
Longfield Clo. PO4 27 G6
Longfield Rd. PO10 22 C2
Longlands Rd. PO10 23 G5
Longmead Gdns. PO9 21 F6
Longs Walk. PO1 26 B4
Longshore Way. PO4 32 C3
Longstock Rd. PO9 15 F5
Longwood Av. PO8 10 D5
Lonsdale Av. PO6 18 D6
Lonsdale Av. PO16 16 C6
Lord Montgomery Way.
  PO5 6 D3
Lordington Clo. PO6 19 E5
Lords St. PO1 26 B5
Lorne Rd. PO5 31 E2
Lovage Way. PO8 8 C6
Lovedean La. PO8 10 C2
Lovett Rd. PO3 25 E4
Lowcay Rd. PO5 30 D4
Lower Bere Wood. PO7 13 F4
Lower Brookfield Rd. PO1 26 C5
Lower Church Path. PO1 6 F2
Lower Derby Rd. PO2 24 B6
Lower Drayton La. PO6 19 E6
Lower Farlington Rd. PO6 19 H5
Lower Forbury Rd. PO5 30 D1
Lower Grove Rd. PO5 21 G5
Lower Rd. PO9 20 B4
Lower Wingfield St. PO1 26 A4
Lowestoft Rd. PO6 18 A4

Lowland Rd. PO7 9 A3
Loxwood Rd. PO8 10 D3
Luard Ct. PO9 21 H4
Lucerne Av. PO7 12 D1
Lucknow St. PO1 26 C6
Ludcombe. PO7 9 B2
Ludlow Rd. PO6 18 A4
Lugano Clo. PO7 12 D2
Lulworth Clo. PO11 34 C2
Lumley Gdns. PO10 23 E5
Lumley Rd. PO10 22 D4
Lumsden Rd. PO4 32 C4
Lutman St. PO10 22 C2
Lych Gate Dri. PO8 11 E1
Lydney Clo. PO6 17 H3
Lymbourn Rd. PO9 21 G4
Lyndhurst Clo. PO11 34 C4
Lyndhurst Rd. PO2 24 D5
Lyne Pl. PO8 11 F3
Lynn Rd. PO2 26 D2
Lynton Gro. PO3 27 F2
Lynwood Av. PO8 10 B6
Lysander Way. PO7 13 G3

Mablethorpe Rd. PO6 18 B4
Macaulay Av. PO6 17 E2
Madeira Rd. PO2 24 D4
Mafeking Rd. PO4 31 F2
Magdala Rd. PO6 18 C6
Magdala Rd. PO11 34 A4
Magdalen Rd. PO2 24 C4
Magnolia Way. PO8 11 F5
Magpie Walk. PO8 10 C5
Maidford Gro. PO3 25 G4
Maidstone Cres. PO6 18 B4
Main Rd, Portsea. PO1 6 A1
Main Rd. PO10 23 E5
Maismore Gdns. PO10 22 B6
Maitland St. PO1 26 B4
Maldon Rd. PO6 18 A5
Malins Rd. PO2 26 B3
Mallard Rd. PO4 27 F6
Mallard Rd. PO9 15 F2
Mallow Clo. PO6 18 C5
Mallow Clo. PO7 13 G5
Malta Rd. PO2 26 C3
Malthouse Rd. PO2 26 B2
Malvern Mews. PO10 22 D4
Malvern Rd. PO5 30 D5
Malwood Clo. PO9 15 F5
Manchester Rd. PO1 26 C6
Manners La. PO4 31 E2
Manners Rd. PO4 31 E2
Manor Clo. PO9 21 F4
Manor Cres. PO6 19 E6
Manor Gdns. PO10 23 G5
Manor Mews. PO6 19 E5
Manor Park Av. PO3 27 E2
Manor Rd. PO11 34 B3
Manor Rd. PO1 26 C4
Manor Rd. PO10 23 G5
Manor Way. PO11 34 C5
Manor Way. PO10 23 G5
Mansion Rd. PO4 31 E5
Mansvid Av. PO6 19 E6
Mantle Sq. PO2 24 A6
Maple Clo. PO16 22 D3
Maple Cres. PO8 8 C2
Maple Dri. PO7 9 C3
Maple Rd. PO5 30 C5
Maple Tree Av. PO8 11 F5
Maralyn Av. PO7 13 F5
Marchwood Rd. PO9 14 C5
Margaret Clo. PO7 13 E2
Margate Rd. PO5 30 C2
Margerys Ct. PO1 6 B3
Marina Clo. PO10 22 D6
Marina Gro. PO3 27 F4
Marina Gro. PO16 16 B5
Marina Keep. PO6 24 A1
Marine Ct. PO4 31 H5
Marine Walk. PO11 35 E4
Mariners Walk. PO4 27 G5
Mariners Way. PO12 28 B5
Marion Rd. PO4 31 E5
Marjoram Cres. PO8 11 F5
Mark Anthony Ct. PO11 34 B4
Mark Clo. PO3 25 E3
Mark Ct. PO7 13 F3

Market Par. PO9 21 F4
Marketway. PO1 6 E1
Markway Clo. PO10 22 B5
*Marlands Lawn,
  Whaddon Ct. PO9 14 B5
Marlborough Clo. PO7 13 E6
Marlborough Gro. PO16 16 B5
Marlborough Park. PO9 21 H2
Marlborough Row. PO1 6 B1
Marldell Clo. PO9 15 F5
Marlowe Ct. PO7 13 E2
Marmion Av. PO5 30 D4
Marmion Rd. PO5 30 C4
Marples Way. PO9 20 D4
Marrels Wood. PO7 19 F1
Marsden Rd. PO6 17 G3
Marsh Clo. PO6 25 G1
Marshall Rd. PO11 35 E5
Marshlands Rd. PC6 19 G6
Marshlands Spur. PO6 19 G6
Marshwood Av. PO7 13 H4
Marston La. PO3 25 G4
Martells Ct. PO1 6 C4
Martin Av. PO7 9 C3
Martin Rd. PO9 21 G1
Martin Rd. PO3 27 E2
Marvic Ct. PO9 14 C5
Masefield Av. PO6 16 D2
Masefield Cres. PO8 10 D5
Matapan Rd. PO2 24 C3
Matthew Clo. PO9 20 C2
Maurepas Way. PO7 13 E4
Maurice Rd. PO4 32 A3
Mavis Cres. PO9 21 F3
Maxstoke Clo. PO5 30 D1
Maxwell Rd. PO4 31 G3
Maydman Sq. PO3 27 E4
Mayfield Rd. PO12 28 A5
Mayfield Rd. PO2 24 D5
Mayflower Dri. PO4 27 G5
Mayhall Rd. PO3 25 E6
Maylands Av. PO4 31 G1
Maylands Rd. PO9 20 B3
Mayles Rd. PO4 27 G6
Maynard Pl. PO8 11 F2
Mayo Clo. PO1 26 B4
Maytree Gdns. PO8 10 C6
Maytree Rd. PO8 10 C6
Meaden Clo. PO9 15 F6
Meadend Rd. PO7 9 B4
Meadow Clo. PO11 36 A2
Meadow Ct. PO10 22 D5
Meadow Edge. PO7 19 E3
Meadow Rise. PO8 11 F5
Meadow St. PO5 30 B2
Meadowlands,
  Havant. PO9 21 G4
Meadowlands,
  Rowlands Castle. PO9 9 C5
Meadowsweet. PO7 14 A2
Meadowsweet Way. PO6 18 A4
Meadway. PO7 13 G2
Meath Clo. PO11 35 E6
Medina Rd. PO6 18 A5
Medstead Rd. PO9 21 F2
Melbourne St. PO5 6 E4
Mellor Clo. PO6 18 A5
Melrose Clo. PO4 32 A3
Melville Rd. PO4 32 B4
Mengham Av. PO11 34 C5
Mengham Ct. PO11 34 C4
Mengham La. PO11 34 C4
Mengham Rd. PO11 34 C4
Meon Clo. PO8 8 C3
Meon Rd. PO4 31 H1
Merchistoun Rd. PO8 11 F2
Mercury Pl. PO7 19 H3
Meredith Rd. PO2 24 D4
Meriden Rd. PO5 6 E4
Merlin Dri. PO3 25 E3
Merlin Gdns. PO16 16 B2
Merrivale Ct. PO10 23 H4
Merrivale Rd. PO2 24 D5
Merrow Clo. PO16 16 A4
Merryfield Av. PO8 14 C6
Merthyr Av. PO6 19 E4
Merton Av. PO16 16 C5
Merton Cres. PO16 16 C5
Merton Rd. PO5 30 C4
Meryl Rd. PO4 32 B3

43

Methuen Rd. PO4 — 31 G3
Mewsey Ct. PO9 — 14 C4
Mey Clo. PO7 — 13 G4
Meyrick Rd. PO9 — 20 D4
Meyrick Rd. PO2 — 24 B6
Michael Crook Clo. PO9 — 20 C2
Midas Ct. PO7 — 19 H1
*Middle Ct,
  George St. PO1 — 26 C3
Middle Park Way. PO9 — 14 B6
Middle St. PO5 — 6 E3
Middlesex Rd. PO4 — 31 H2
Middleton Rise. PO8 — 8 C3
Midway Rd. PO2 — 24 D3
Milbeck Clo. PO8 — 11 E6
Mile End Rd. PO2 — 26 A4
Milebush Rd. PO4 — 27 G6
Milford Clo. PO9 — 20 D2
Milford Rd. PO1 — 26 B6
Military Rd. PO3 — 24 D2
Military Rd. PO1 — 29 G1
Milk La F.P. PO7. — 12 D5
Mill Clo. PO7 — 9 C3
Mill End. PO10 — 23 E5
Mill La, Bedhampton. PO9 — 20 C4
Mill La, Langstone. PO9 — 21 F6
Mill La. PO10 — 23 E4
Mill La. PO7 — 18 B3
Mill La. PO1 — 26 A4
Mill Quay. PO10 — 23 E6
Mill Rd. Denmead. PO7 — 9 C3
Mill Rd, Waterlooville. PO7 — 13 E5
Mill Rd. PO10 — 23 F1
Mill Rythe La. PO11 — 36 B6
Millbrook Dri. PO9 — 15 E5
Mills Rd. PO2 — 26 B2
Milton La. PO3 — 26 D6
Milton Parade. PO7 — 13 E1
Milton Park Av. PO4 — 31 H2
Milton Rd. PO3 — 27 E4
Milton Rd. PO7 — 13 E2
Minerva Clo. PO7 — 19 H3
Minley Ct. PO9 — 15 F6
Minstead Rd. PO4 — 32 A4
Minters Lepe. PO7 — 19 G2
Mission La. PO8 — 10 D6
Mitchell Rd. PO9 — 20 C2
Mitchell Way. PO3 — 25 G4
Mole Hill. PO7 — 13 G6
Molesworth Rd. PO12 — 28 A5
Monarch Clo. PO7 — 13 G4
Monckton Rd. PO3 — 25 E5
Moneyfields Av. PO3 — 27 E2
Moneyfields La. PO3 — 27 E2
Monks Hill. PO10 — 23 E1
Monkwood Clo. PO9 — 14 B6
Monmouth Clo. PO7 — 13 G4
Monmouth Rd. PO2 — 24 C6
Montague Rd. PO2 — 24 C6
Montana Ct. PO7 — 13 G5
Monteray Dri. PO9 — 21 G1
Montgomerie Rd. PO5 — 30 D2
Montgomery Rd. PO9 — 21 G4
Montgomery Walk. PO7 — 13 G4
Monton Ct. PO9 — 15 F5
Montrose Av. PO16 — 16 D2
Monument La. PO17 — 16 B1
*Monxton Grn,
  Burghclere Rd. PO9 — 15 F5
Moor Park. PO7 — 14 A2
Moorgreen Rd. PO9 — 15 E6
Moorings Way. PO4 — 27 G5
Moorland Rd. PO1 — 26 C5
Moortown Av. PO6 — 19 F4
Moraunt Dri. PO16 — 16 A5
Morelands Ct. PO7 — 19 H1
Morelands Rd. PO7 — 19 G1
Morgan Rd. PO4 — 32 A3
Morley Cres. PO8 — 11 E5
Morley Rd. PO4 — 31 G4
Morningside Av. PO16 — 16 D3
Mortimer Rd. PO6 — 17 G3
Mortimers Lawn. PO9 — 14 C4
Mosdell Rd. PO10 — 23 H6
Moulin Av. PO5 — 31 E4
Mount View Av. PO16 — 16 D3
Mountbatten Dri. PO7 — 12 D5
Mountwood Rd. PO10 — 23 H4
Mousehole Rd. PO6 — 17 E3
Muccleshell Clo. PO9 — 21 G1

Mulberry Av. PO6 — 18 D6
Mulberry La. PO6 — 18 D6
Mulberry Path. PO6 — 18 D6
Mullion Clo. PO6 — 17 G5
Mumby Rd. PO12 — 28 B3
Mundays Row. PO8 — 8 C6
Munster Rd. PO2 — 24 C5
Murefield St. PO1 — 26 B6
Muriel Rd. PO7 — 13 F3
Murray Rd. PO8 — 11 F3
Murrays La. PO1 — 6 A1
*Murrel Gdns,
  Tunbulm Ct. PO9 — 15 F6
*Murrell Grn,
  Meaden Clo. PO9 — 15 F6
Muscliffe Ct. PO9 — 15 F5
Museum Rd. PO1 — 30 A2
My Lords La. PO — 34 D4
Myrtle Av. PO16 — 16 C4
Myrtle Gro. PO3 — 27 F4

Nailsworth Rd. PO6 — 17 G3
Naish Ct. PO9 — 14 B4
Nancy Rd. PO1 — 26 C6
Napier Rd. PO8 — 11 G2
Napier Rd. PO5 — 30 D4
Narvik Rd. PO2 — 24 C3
Naseby Clo. PO6 — 17 F3
Navy Rd. PO1 — 29 F1
Neelands Gro. PO6 — 16 D4
Nelson Av. PO2 — 24 C5
Nelson Av. PO16 — 16 A4
Nelson Cres. PO8 — 11 F2
Nelson Rd. PO17 — 16 B1
Nelson Rd. PO1 — 26 A4
Nelson Rd. PO5 — 30 C3
Nerissa Clo. PO7 — 13 H2
Nessus St. PO2 — 26 B2
Netherfield Clo. PO9 — 21 G4
Netley Rd. PO5 — 30 C4
Netley Ter. PO5 — 30 C4
Nettlecombe Av. PO4 — 31 E5
Nettlestone Rd. PO4 — 31 G4
Neville Av. PO16 — 16 C5
Neville Gdns. PO10 — 22 C2
Neville Rd. PO3 — 27 F4
Neville Shute Rd. PO3 — 25 F4
New Brighton Rd. PO10 — 22 D4
New Cut. PO11 — 36 A2
New Down La. PO7 — 18 D3
New La. PO9 — 21 G3
New Rd, Clanfield. PO8 — 8 C3
New Rd, Havant. PO9 — 20 D3
New Rd, Lovedean. PO8 — 10 C2
New Rd, Portsmouth. PO2 — 26 C3
New Rd,
  Southbourne. PO10 — 23 H5
New Rd, Westbourne. PO10 — 23 E2
New Rd East. PO2 — 26 D3
Newbarn Rd. PO9 — 20 C2
Newbolt Gdns. PO8 — 10 C5
Newbolt Rd. PO6 — 16 D3
Newcome Rd. PO1 — 26 C5
Newcomen Rd. PO2 — 24 B6
Newlands La. PO7 — 12 B3
Newlands Rd. PO7 — 13 E6
Newlease Rd. PO7 — 13 F6
Newlyn Way. PO6 — 17 F4
Newmer Ct. PO9 — 14 B5
Newney Clo. PO2 — 25 E4
Newnham Ct. PO9 — 15 F6
Newtown. PO16 — 16 C4
Newtown La. PO11 — 34 A3
Nicholas Clo. PO11 — 34 A4
Nicholson Way. PO9 — 21 E2
Nickel St. PO5 — 30 B3
Nickleby Rd. PO8 — 8 B1
Nightjar Clo. PO8 — 11 E2
Nightingale Clo. PO9 — 15 F2
Nightingale Pk. PO9 — 21 H4
Nightingale Rd. PO5 — 30 B4
Nile St. PO10 — 22 D6
Ninian Park Rd. PO3 — 25 E5
Ninian Path. PO3 — 25 E5
Nobbs La. PO1 — 6 C4
Nore Cres. PO10 — 22 B5
Nore Farm Av. PO10 — 22 B4
Norfolk Cres. PO11 — 34 A5
Norfolk St. PO5 — 30 B2
Norgett Way. PO16 — 16 B5

Norland Rd. PO4 — 31 E2
Norley Clo. PO9 — 14 C6
Norman Rd. PO16 — 16 C5
Norman Rd. PO11 — 34 D5
Norman Rd. PO4 — 31 E3
Norman Way. PO9 — 20 C3
Normandy Rd. PO2 — 24 C3
Norris Gdns. PO9 — 21 G5
North Av. PO2 — 24 D2
North Battery Rd. PO2 — 24 A5
North Clo. PO9 — 21 G5
*North Ct, George St. PO2 — 26 C3
North Cres. PO11 — 34 D4
North Cross St. PO12 — 28 C4
North End Av. PO2 — 24 C5
North End Gro. PO2 — 24 C5
North La. PO8 — 8 B1
North Rd. PO8 — 8 C5
North Shore Rd. PO11 — 33 H3
North St,
  Bedhampton. PO9 — 20 D3
North St, Emsworth. PO1 — 22 D4
North St, Gosport. PO12 — 28 B3
North St, Havant. PO9 — 21 F4
North St, Portsea. PO1 — 6 C2
North St, Portsmouth. PO1 — 26 B4
North St,
  Westbourne. PO10 — 23 E2
North Way. PO9 — 21 E4
Northam Mews. PO1 — 26 B5
Northam St. PO1 — 26 B5
Northarbour Path. PO6 — 18 A5
Northarbour Rd. PO6 — 18 A6
Northarbour Spur. PO6 — 18 A5
Northbrook Clo. PO1 — 26 B4
Northcote Rd. PO4 — 31 E3
Northern Par. PO2 — 24 C4
Northern Rd. PO6 — 18 C6
Northfield Clo. PO8 — 8 C4
Northfield Pk. PO16 — 16 A3
Northgate Av. PO2 — 26 D3
Northney La. PO11 — 36 C1
Northney Rd. PO11 — 36 B1
Northover Rd. PO3 — 27 F2
Northumberland Rd. PO1 — 31 E1
Northwood La. PO11 — 36 B4
Northwood Rd. PO2 — 24 D3
Norton Clo. PO7 — 13 E4
Norway Rd. PO3 — 25 E3
Norwich Rd. PO6 — 18 A4
Novello Gdns. PO7 — 13 F5
Nursery Clo. PO10 — 22 D2
Nursery Gdns. PO8 — 11 E4
Nursery Rd. PO9 — 20 C3
Nursling Cres. PO9 — 15 F6
Nutbourne Rd. PO6 — 19 G6
Nutbourne Rd. PO11 — 35 G6
Nutfield Pl. PO1 — 26 B4
Nuthatch Clo. PO9 — 15 F2
Nutley Rd. PO9 — 14 C6
Nutwick Rd. PO9 — 21 H2
Nyewood Av. PO16 — 16 C2
Nyria Wk. PO12 — 28 B4

O'Jays Ind Pk. PO3 — 25 F6
Oak Clo. PO8 — 13 F1
Oak Park Dri. PO9 — 21 G2
Oak Rd. PO8 — 8 C2
Oak St. PO12 — 28 A4
Oak Tree Dri. PO10 — 22 C1
Oakapple Gdns. PO6 — 19 H5
Oakfield Clo. PO9 — 15 F6
Oakhurst Dri. PO7 — 13 G3
Oakhurst Gdns. PO7 — 19 E3
Oaklands Gro. PO8 — 10 C5
Oaklands Rd. PO9 — 21 G4
Oaklea Clo. PO7 — 19 E3
Oakley Rd. PO9 — 14 C6
Oakmeadow Clo. PO10 — 22 D2
Oakmont. PO8 — 13 G1
Oaks Coppice. PO8 — 11 E3
Oakshott Dri. PO9 — 15 E5
Oakwood Av. PO9 — 20 B2
Oakwood Rd. PO9 — 34 B4
Oakwood Rd. PO2 — 24 D3
Oberon Clo. PO7 — 13 G3
Ocean Park
  Shopping Centre. PO3 — 25 F6
Ockenden Clo. PO5 — 6 E4
Octavius Ct. PO7 — 13 H2

Old Barn Gdns. PO8 — 10 D3
Old Bridge Rd. PO4 — 31 E4
Old Commercial Rd. PO1 — 26 A4
Old Copse Rd. PO9 — 21 G2
Old Farm La. PO10 — 23 F3
Old Farm Way. PO6 — 19 H6
Old Gate Gdns. PO2 — 24 D4
Old La. PO8 — 8 B5
Old London Rd. PO2 — 25 E3
Old Manor Way. PO6 — 18 D6
Old Rectory Clo. PO10 — 23 E2
Old Rectory Rd. PO6 — 19 H5
Old Reservoir Rd. PO6 — 19 G6
Old River. PO7 — 9 B3
Old Road. PO12 — 28 A5
Old School Dri. PO11 — 34 D5
Old Star Pl. PO1 — 6 B2
Old Timbers. PO11 — 34 B4
Old Van Diemans Rd. PO7 — 12 D6
Old Wymering La. PO6 — 18 B5
Olinda St. PO1 — 26 C5
Olive Cres. PO16 — 16 C5
Oliver Rd. PO4 — 31 G3
Olivia Clo. PO7 — 13 H2
Omega St. PO5 — 30 D1
Onslow Rd. PO5 — 30 D5
Ophir Rd. PO2 — 24 C5
Oracle Dri. PO7 — 19 H2
Orange Row. PO10 — 22 D6
Orchard Clo. PO8 — 11 G3
Orchard Gro. PO8 — 10 D6
Orchard Gro. PO16 — 16 A5
Orchard La. PO9 — 23 E5
Orchard Rd. PO9 — 21 F5
Orchard Rd. PO11 — 34 C5
Orchard Rd. PO4 — 31 E1
Ordnance Ct. PO3 — 25 F3
Ordnance Rd. PO12 — 28 B4
Ordnance Row. PO1 — 6 B3
Oriel Rd. PO2 — 24 C5
Orkney Rd. PO6 — 18 C4
Ormsby Rd. PO5 — 30 C4
Orsmond Clo. PO7 — 13 F5
Osborne Clo. PO7 — 13 G4
Osborne Rd. PO5 — 30 B4
Osprey Clo. PO6 — 19 H6
Osprey Dri. PO11 — 34 D4
Osprey Quay. PO10 — 23 E4
Othello Dri. PO7 — 13 G3
Otterbourne Cres. PO9 — 14 C6
Outram Rd. PO5 — 30 D1
Overton Cres. PO9 — 14 B4
Overton Rd. PO10 — 23 H1
Owen St. PO4 — 31 G1
Owslebury Gro. PO9 — 14 D6
Oxenwood Grn. PO9 — 14 B6
Oxford Rd. PO5 — 31 E4
Oxted Ct. PO4 — 27 G6
Oyster Mews. PO1 — 29 F1
Oyster Quay. PO6 — 17 G3
Oyster St. PO1 — 29 F1

Padbury Clo. PO2 — 25 E5
Paddington Rd. PO2 — 26 D6
Paddock End. PO7 — 9 B5
Paddock Walk. PO6 — 17 E5
Padnell Av. PO8 — 11 E4
Padnell Pl. PO8 — 11 F4
Padnell Rd. PO8 — 11 E4
Padwick Av. PO6 — 18 D4
Pagham Clo. PO10 — 23 E1
Pagham Gdns. PO11 — 35 G6
Paignton Av. PO3 — 27 E3
Pains Rd. PO5 — 30 C1
Painswick Clo. PO6 — 25 G4
Painter Clo. PO3 — 25 G4
Palk Rd. PO9 — 20 D1
Palmers Rd. PO10 — 22 D1
Palmerston Rd. PO11 — 34 C5
Palmerston Rd. PO5 — 30 C1
Pamela Av. PO6 — 17 F3
Pan St. PO1 — 6 F4
Pangbourne Av. PO6 — 18 D4
Panton Clo. PO10 — 22 C1
Paradise La. PO10 — 23 E1
Paradise St. PO1 — 6 F4
Parham Rd. PO12 — 28 A4
Park Av. PO7 — 19 E3
Park Cres. PO10 — 22 B4
Park Farm Rd. PO7 — 19 F3

45

St Christophers Rd. PO9 20 C2
St Clares Av. PO9 14 B4
St Colmans Av. PO6 18 D5
St Davids Rd. PO8 8 C3
St Davids Rd. PO5 30 D2
*St Denys Walk,
  Stanswood Rd. PO9 14 C5
St Edwards Rd. PO5 30 B3
St Faiths Rd. PO1 6 F1
St Francis Pl. PO9 21 E2
St Georges Av. PO9 21 H4
St Georges Rd. PO6 18 C5
St Georges Rd. PO4 31 G5
St Georges Rd. PO11 33 H4
St Georges Rd. PO1 6 C3
St Georges Sq. PO1 6 C3
St Georges Walk. PO7 13 E4
St Georges Way. PO1 6 C3
St Giles Way. PO8 8 C5
St Helena Way. PO16 16 B4
St Helens Clo. PO4 31 F5
St Helens Par. PO4 31 E5
St Helens Park Cres. PO4 31 E5
St Helens Rd. PO6 19 F5
St Helens Rd. PO11 33 H4
St Hermans Rd. PO11 35 E5
St Hilda Av. PO8 8 C5
St Hubert Rd. PO8 8 C5
St James Clo. PO8 8 C3
St James Rd. PO10 22 D5
St James's Rd. PO5 6 E4
St James's St. PO1 6 C2
St James Way. PO16 16 B4
St Johns Av. PO7 19 G1
St Johns Clo. PO11 34 B4
St Johns Rd. PO6 18 C5
St Johns Rd. PO9 20 C1
St Johns Rd. PO10 23 G5
St Judes Clo. PO5 30 C4
St Leonards Av. PO11 34 C3
St Margarets Rd. PO11 34 C4
St Marks Rd. PO2 24 C6
St Marys Rd. PO11 34 C3
St Marys Rd. PO1 26 C4
St Matthews Rd. PO6 18 C5
St Michaels Rd. PO9 20 C1
St Michaels Rd. PO1 6 D3
St Michaels Way. PO8 8 C5
St Nicholas Rd. PO9 20 C2
St Nicholas St. PO1 30 A3
St Pauls Rd. PO5 6 D4
St Pauls Sq. PO5 6 D4
St Peters Av. PO11 36 C3
St Peters Gro. PO5 30 C3
St Peters Rd. PO11 36 C2
St Peters Sq. PO10 22 D5
St Pirans Av. PO3 27 E3
St Ronans Av. PO4 31 E4
St Ronans Rd. PO4 31 E5
St Simons Rd. PO5 30 D5
St Stephens Rd. PO2 26 C2
St Swithuns Rd. PO2 25 E5
St Theresas Clo. PO9 20 D2
St Thomas Av. PO11 33 H4
St Thomas's Ct. PO1 30 A3
St Thomas's St. PO1 6 C4
St Ursula Gro. PO5 30 D3
St Vincent Cres. PO8 11 F2
St Vincent Rd. PO5 30 D4
St Vincent St. PO5 6 E3
Salcombe Av. PO3 27 F2
Salerno Rd. PO2 24 C3
Salet Way. PO7 14 A2
Salisbury Rd. PO6 18 D6
Salisbury Rd. PO4 31 F4
Salterns Av. PO4 27 F5
Salterns Clo. PO11 35 E4
Salterns La. PO11 35 E4
Saltmarsh La. PO11 34 A2
Salvia Clo. PO7 13 G5
Sampson Rd. PO1 6 A1
Samuel Rd. PO1 26 D5
Sandalwood Clo. PO8 8 C2
Sanderling Rd. PO4 27 H6
Sandleford Rd. PO9 14 C4
Sandown Rd. PO6 18 B6
Sandpiper Clo. PO8 11 E2
Sandpipers. PO6 19 H6
Sandport Gro. PO16 16 A5
Sandringham La. PO1 26 C6

Sandringham Rd. PO1 26 C5
Sandy Beach Estate. PO11 35 G6
Sandy Brow. PO7 19 G2
Sandy Point Rd. PO11 35 F6
Sandyfield Cres. PO8 10 C6
Sapphire Ridge. PO7 13 H4
Saxley Ct. PO9 14 B5
Saxon Clo. PO8 8 G4
Saxon Clo. PO16 16 B2
Scholars Walk. PO6 19 E6
School La,
  Emsworth. PO10 22 D5
School La,
  Westbourne. PO10 23 E1
School Rd. PO9 21 E4
Schooner Way. PO4 27 H5
Scotney Ct. PO9 15 F5
Scott Rd. PO3 25 E2
Scott Rd. PO1 6 A2
Scratchface La. PO9 20 A1
Sea Front Estate. PO11 34 D5
Sea Horse Walk. PO12 28 C3
Sea Mill Gdns. PO1 6 C3
Sea View Rd. PO6 19 F5
Sea View Rd. PO11 35 E4
Seafield Rd. PO3 25 E6
Seafield Rd. PO16 16 A5
Seafields. PO10 22 C6
Seafront. PO11 34 A4
Seagers Ct. PO1 29 E5
Seagrove Av. PO11 34 C5
Seagrove Rd. PO2 26 B1
Seagull Clo. PO4 27 H5
Seagull La. PO10 22 D5
Seaton Av. PO3 27 F2
Seaview Av. PO16 16 D3
Seaview Ter. PO10 22 D6
Seaview Ter. PO11 33 H4
Seaward Tower. PO12 28 C4
Seaway Cres. PO4 32 B3
Seaway Gro. PO16 16 B5
Sebastion Gro. PO7 13 G3
Second Av, Cosham. PO6 18 B5
Second Av, Drayton. PO6 19 G6
Second Av. PO9 21 H3
Second Av. PO10 23 G5
Sedgefield Clo. PO6 16 D4
Sedgeley Clo. PO5 6 F4
Selangor A.v. PO10 22 A5
Selbourne Av. PO9 14 B6
Selbourne Rd. PO9 21 E4
Selbourne Ter. PO1 26 C6
Selsey Av. PO4 31 G5
Selsey Clo. PO11 35 H5
Selsmore Av. PO11 35 E5
Selsmore Rd. PO11 34 C4
Sennen Pl. PO6 17 F4
Sentinel Clo. PO7 13 H2
Serpentine Rd. PO7 19 F2
Serpentine Rd,
  Southsea. PO5 30 B5
Serpentine Rd,
  Southsea. PO5 30 C4
Settlers Clo. PO1 6 F2
Sevenoaks Rd. PO6 18 B5
Severn Clo. PO6 17 G2
Seymour Clo. PO2 26 B3
Shadwell Rd. PO2 24 C5
Shaftesbury Av. PO7 13 E6
Shaftesbury Rd. PO12 28 A4
Shaftesbury Rd. PO5 30 B4
Shakespeare Gdns. PO8 10 C5
Shakespeare Rd. PO1 26 C4
Shaldon Rd. PO9 15 F5
Shamrock Clo. PO12 28 B4
Shanklin Rd. PO4 31 E2
Sharps Clo. PO3 25 F4
Sharps Rd. PO9 15 F6
Shawcross Ind Pk. PO3 25 F2
Shawfield Rd. PO9 21 G5
Shawford Clo. PO9 14 A6
Shearer Rd. PO1 26 C3
Shearwater Dri. PO6 19 H6
Sheepwash La. PO7 12 A2
Sheepwash Rd. PO8 11 G4
Sheffield Rd. PO1 26 C5
Shelford Rd. PO4 27 F6
Shelley Av. PO6 16 D3
Shelley Gdns. PO8 10 C5
Sheppard Clo. PO8 11 E2

Sherfield Av. PO9 15 E6
Sheringham Rd. PO6 18 A4
Shetland Clo. PO6 18 C4
Shillinglee. PO7 19 H2
Ship Leopard St. PO1 6 B3
Shipton Grn. PO9 14 B5
Shire Clo. PO7 14 A2
Shirley Av. PO4 32 A3
Shirley Rd. PO5 31 E4
Sholing Ct. PO9 14 C5
Shore Av. PO4 27 G5
Shore Haven. PO6 17 E4
Shorelands Ct. PO11 35 G6
Short Row. PO1 6 B1
Shrubbery Clo. PO16 16 B5
Sidlesham Clo. PO11 35 G5
Sidmouth Av. PO3 27 F2
Silchester Rd. PO3 27 F3
Silkstead Av. PO9 14 D5
Silver St. PO5 30 B3
Silverdale Rd. PO7 10 B6
Silverlock Clo. PO2 26 A2
Silversands Gdns. PO11 34 D5
Silverthorne Way. PO7 12 D3
Silvertrees. PO10 22 D3
Silvester Rd. PO8 10 C6
Simmons Grn. PO11 34 D4
Simpson Clo. PO16 16 B3
Simpson Rd. PO2 24 B6
Simpson Rd. PO6 18 C4
Sinah La. PO11 33 G4
Singleton Gdns. PO8 8 D3
Siskin Gro. PO7 13 H5
Sissinghurst Rd. PO16 16 A5
Sixth Av. PO6 18 B5
Skew Rd. PO17 16 B2
Slater App. PO2 24 A6
Slindon Clo. PO8 8 C3
Slindon Gdns. PO9 21 F5
Slindon St. PO1 6 F2
Slingsby Clo. PO1 30 B3
Slipper Rd. PO10 23 E6
Smallcuts Av. PO10 23 G4
Smeaton St. PO2 24 B6
Snowberry Cres. PO9 21 H2
Soake Rd. PO7 9 D4
Soberton Rd. PO9 21 E2
Soldridge Clo. PO9 15 G5
Solent Dri. PO11 34 B4
Solent Rd, Drayton. PO6 19 F5
Solent Rd, Havant. PO9 21 E4
Solent Vw. PO16 16 B3
Somborne Dri. PO9 14 D6
Somers Rd. PO5 6 F4
Somers Rd North. PO1 26 B6
Somerset Rd. PO5 30 D5
Somerville Pl. PO2 24 B5
Sonnet Way. PO7 13 H2
Sopley Ct. PO9 15 F5
Sorrel Clo. PO7 13 H5
South Av. PO2 24 D3
South Clo. PO9 21 G5
South Cross St. PO12 28 C4
South La. PO8 8 A2
South La. PO10 23 H3
South Normandy. PO1 6 C4
South Parade. PO5 30 D6
South Rd. PO8 8 C6
South Rd. PO6 19 F6
South Rd. PO11 34 B4
South St. PO1 26 C4
South St. PO10 22 D6
South St. PO12 28 A5
South St. PO9 21 F5
South St. PO5 30 B2
South Ter. PO1 6 B2
South View Clo. PO8 11 E5
Southampton Rd. PO6 18 A5
Southampton Row. PO1 6 B2
Southbourne Av. PO6 19 E6
Southbourne Av. PO10 23 F5
Southbrook Clo. PO9 21 F5
Southbrook Rd. PO9 21 F5
Southdown Rd
  Catherington. PO8 8 B5
Southdown Rd. PO8 8 C4
Southdown Rd. PO6 18 D5
Southdown Vw. PO7 12 D1
Southfield Walk. PO9 14 B4
Southleigh Gro. PO11 34 B3

Southleigh Rd. PO9 21 H4
Southmoor La. PO9 20 D6
Southsea Esplanade. PO4 31 E6
Southsea Ter. PO5 30 B3
Southwick Av. PO16 16 D2
Southwick Hill Rd. PO6 18 A3
Southwick Rd. PO6 17 G1
Southwick Rd. PO7 9 A3
Southwood Rd. PO11 35 E5
Southwood Rd. PO2 24 D4
Sovereign Clo. PO4 27 H5
Sovereign Dri. PO4 27 H5
Sovereign La. PO7 19 G2
Sparrow Clo. PO8 10 D4
Sparsholt Clo. PO9 14 A6
Specks La. PO4 31 G1
Spencer Clo. PO11 34 C4
Spencer Gdrs. PO8 10 D5
Spencer Rd. PO10 22 C2
Spencer Rd. PO4 31 F5
Spenlow Clo. PO2 26 B3
Spicer St. PO1 6 F1
Spindle Clo. PO9 22 A3
Spindle Warren. PO9 22 A3
Spinnaker Clo. PO11 34 B3
Spinnaker Dri. PO2 24 C3
Spinnaker Grange. PO11 36 D1
Spinnaker View. PO9 20 B4
Spinney Clo. PO8 10 C5
Spring Garden La. PO12 28 B4
Spring Gdns. PO10 22 D5
Spring Gdns. PO1 6 E3
Spring St. PO1 6 E2
Spring Vale. PO8 11 F5
Springfield Clo. PO9 20 B3
Springwood Av. PO7 13 G5
Spruce Av. PO7 13 G4
Spur Rd. PO6 18 C5
Spur Rd. PO7 13 F4
Stacey Ct. PO9 14 B4
Stafford Rd. PO5 30 D3
Stagshorn Rd. PO8 11 G1
Stakes Hill Rd. PO7 13 F4
Stakes Rd. PO7 19 F1
Stallard Clo. PO10 22 C5
Stamford Av. PO11 34 A4
Stamford St. PO1 26 C5
Stamshaw Prom. PO2 24 C3
Stamshaw Rd . PO2 24 C5
Stanbridge Rd. PO9 21 H2
Standford Ct. PO9 15 F6
Stanford Clo. PO6 18 A5
Stanhope Rd. PO1 6 E2
Stanley Av. PO3 27 F2
Stanley La. PO1 30 C4
Stanley Rd. PO10 22 D6
Stanley Rd. PO2 24 B6
Stanley St. PO5 30 C4
Stanstead Rd. PO5 15 G1
Stanstead Rd. PO5 30 D2
Stansted Cres. PO9 15 F5
Stanswood Rd. PO9 14 C5
Staple Clo. PO7 13 E1
Stapleton Rd. PO3 27 E2
Starina Gdns. PO7 14 A2
Station Rd. PO3 27 E3
Station Rd. PO6 19 F6
Station Rd. PO11 34 A3
Station Rd. PO16 16 C3
Station St. PO1 6 E2
Staunton Av. PO11 33 H4
Staunton Rd. PO9 21 E3
Staunton St. PO1 26 A4
Stead Clo. PO11 34 D4
Steel St. PO5 30 B3
Steep Clo. PO16 16 B2
Steerforth Clo. PO2 26 A3
Stein Rd. PO10 23 G3
Stephen Clo. PO7 14 A1
Stewart Pl. PO1 26 C3
Stirling Av. PO7 13 G4
Stirling St. PO2 26 B3
Stock Heath La. PO9 21 E3
Stock Heath Rd. PO9 21 F1
Stock Heath Way. PO9 21 F2
Stockbridge Clo. PO9 15 F6
Stoke Gdns. PO12 28 A4
Stoke Rd. PO12 28 A4
Stone Sq. PO9 21 F1
Stone St. PO5 30 B3